12/22/16

GAME OF
MY LIFE

SAN DIEGO

CHARGERS

To Kody —
The Chargers are <u>lucky</u>
to have you for a fan!

Go Bolts Go!
Jay Paris

GAME OF MY LIFE

SAN DIEGO

CHARGERS

MEMORABLE STORIES OF CHARGERS FOOTBALL

JAY PARIS

Foreword by Dick Enberg

SPORTS
PUBLISHING

Sports Publishing books may be purchased in bulk at special discounts for sales promotion, corporate gifts, fund-raising, or educational purposes. Special editions can also be created to specifications. For details, contact the Special Sales Department, Sports Publishing, 307 West 36th Street, 11th Floor, New York, NY 10018 or sportspubbooks@skyhorsepublishing.com.

Sports Publishing® is a registered trademark of Skyhorse Publishing, Inc.®, a Delaware corporation.

Visit our website at www.sportspubbooks.com.

10 9 8 7 6 5 4 3 2 1

Library of Congress Cataloging-in-Publication Data is available on file.

Interior photos courtesy of the San Diego Chargers.

Cover design by Tom Lau
Cover photo credit by AP Images

ISBN: 978-1-61321-921-8
Ebook ISBN: 978-1-61321-922-5
Printed in the United States of America

CONTENTS

FOREWORD

By Dick Enberg

When reading through *Game of My Life San Diego Chargers*, I'm richly reminded of how many special and unique moments the team has produced through its heartwarming, as well as its heartbreaking, history.

Turning the pages in this book is like flipping through countless Chargers memories: some bring a championship smile while others elicit a what-might-have-been frown.

But that's the beauty of football. And the tales of these Chargers' most significant games—for one reason or another—reveal a different perspective of what transpired during those timeless outings.

From Paul Lowe returning the AFL Chargers' first kickoff for a touchdown, to Ron Mix wrestling with the Rams' Deacon Jones in their heated helmet-to-helmet combat along the line.

From Lance Alworth gracefully gliding through the air to snag another reception (which illustrated why he was called "Bambi"), to Doug "Moosie" Wilkerson providing protection for yet another Dan Fouts touchdown strike.

Ed White talks of the Freezer Bowl, when the Chargers fell to the Cincinnati Bengals in the 1981 AFC Championship Game. With the wind chill, the temperature read minus fifty-nine degrees, and I'm still waiting for my toes to thaw from broadcasting that game with Merlin Olsen.

In fact, Fouts still suffers from frostbite on the fingers of his throwing hand.

I'm reminded of the dramatic seconds in Pittsburgh as I called Dennis Gibson deflecting Neil O'Donnell's pass that advanced the Chargers to their lone Super Bowl.

And I still get goose bumps (not to mention inspired) when reliving a sickly, but courageous, Rolf Benirschke gingerly walking to midfield for the coin flip against the Pittsburgh Steelers. It was an emotional day with many thinking in the broadcast booth, and throughout San Diego Stadium, it was Benirschke's last time on a football field.

Football was always fun when LaDainian Tomlinson had the ball tucked under his arm near the goal line. You'll bounce along with L. T. to the outside of the Denver Broncos' run defense as he collects his record-breaking, single-season rushing touchdown.

Jay Paris, a longtime San Diego sportswriter, brings to light so many compelling stories. His coverage of the Chargers coincided with coach Bobby Ross's arrival in 1992. Few know the Chargers as well as Paris, and he proves it in this fast-moving book.

So take a seat at the 50-yard line and enjoy the incredible Chargers memories, chronicled by one of our finest writers.

Chapter 1

PAUL LOWE

Titans at Chargers—August 6, 1960

BIRTH DATE:	September 27, 1936
HOMETOWN:	Homer, Louisiana
RESIDENCE:	San Diego, California
JERSEY NO.:	23
POSITION:	Running back/kick returner
HEIGHT:	6-foot-0
WEIGHT:	205 pounds

The Run-up

Paul Lowe wasn't seeking gold in 1959 with the San Francisco 49ers; he just wanted a job.

Lowe had caught the eye of a 49ers official when playing at Oregon State. One day the scout slipped him a card, telling Lowe San Francisco might be interested when he was done being a scatback with the Beavers.

"He pulled me to the side and told me to get in touch," Lowe said.

Lowe did just that and got a look by the 49ers.

"Red Hickey was the coach and he said I did really good," he said.

But in a preseason game, Lowe went around the end. There's still debate on which hole wasn't blocked, but the result was Lowe's shoulder taking the brunt of a linebacker's blow.

"He knocked the hell out of me," Lowe said. "He really clocked me and dislocated my shoulder. Well, the 49ers were having a cut-down and so they cut me."

A man who would go on to lead the AFL in rushing in five of his first seven seasons was unemployed.

The player later known for his speed went about selling fast cars for a living. Hawking Dodges and Chryslers was pretty neat, but Lowe sought something more substantial to support his family.

While searching for another line of work, he borrowed one of the vehicles from his old used-car lot. Intrigued by law enforcement, he applied for a position with the Los Angeles Police Department.

"I went to take the test and I did well," Lowe said. "But they did a background check on me. They found out the car that I drove down to take the test had gotten a ticket.

"They said, 'We like your application, but it says here you have a warrant on a ticket.' I said, 'Well I don't own the car.'"

Lowe's pleas for leniency were met with a shrug.

"Well, you were the person driving it," was the officer's reply.

Talk about an interview taking a wrong turn.

"They took me to jail," Lowe said, in a voice that was a mix of laughter and exasperation. "I come in to take the test and they put me in jail. I call my mom and she said, 'What are you doing in jail? I thought you were going to become a policeman.' I told her about the ticket on the car I was driving.

"We were poor. She didn't have any money to get me out of jail. But somehow she rounded some up and got me out. That was my mom, rest in peace. I made it up to her before she passed away."

His episode with the LAPD behind him, Lowe latched on with Carte Blanche credit, a division of Hilton Hotels. It was run by Barron Hilton, the future owner of the L.A. Chargers, as well as grandfather of Paris Hilton.

Lowe was hired to toil in the mail room. On work days, Lowe punched in at the Santa Monica Hilton, with his football-playing dreams all but forgotten.

"I was working for Frank Leahy, the old Notre Dame coach," Lowe said. "He came up to me one day and said him and Hilton were going to start a new football team in L.A. He heard from the guys that I had done really well as a running back and on special teams. He wanted to know if I would like to play. He turned out to be the first general manager of the Chargers.

"I said, 'Yeah, I sure would like to play.' Then Sid Gillman got in touch with me and signed me to play football. He had seen me play with the 49ers when he had coached the Rams."

Carte Blanche's loss was a gain for the Chargers and the newfangled endeavor called the American Football League.

"Frank Leahy didn't stay there much longer after we had our talk," Lowe said.

Neither did Lowe.

The Game

By Paul Lowe

The first one that jumps out for me was when I became a professional football player for the Los Angeles Chargers. It was against the then-New York Titans in an exhibition game at the L.A. Coliseum, the first game the Chargers ever played in the American Football League.

I was on the kickoff return team and I returned it for 105 yards. I went up the middle and headed toward the sideline and took it all on that way. That was the happiest I had ever been and that is why the Chargers kept me.

It was comical because there was hardly anybody there; they should have made a movie out of it. They had to move all the people to one side of the stadium to make it look like a lot of people were at the game.

The Rams were the team that was drawing all the people back then. So the people that came to that first game they put them all behind our bench. They didn't show anything on the other side because there [were] no other people. And the people that were in there, they probably sneaked in.

That we even had a team was something.

When we had a tryout there, we must have had 2,000 people trying to make the Chargers. Everyone from people in the movies to plumbers, carpenters, shoe-shine boys, and real notable players like Ron Waller. We had a bunch of movie stars trying out. They wanted to have some movie stars to put on the sidelines, but these guys wanted to be linebackers.

But for that first game, that was why that return was so important because I knew I had to beat out Ron Waller.

At that time Sid Gillman was the coach, but he had been the coach of the L.A. Rams and one of his players was Ron Waller and he was on kickoffs, too.

So I had to beat out Ron Waller and sure there was favoritism. Waller was one of Sid's guys.

In our last exhibition game, I was on kickoff return again, me and Ron Waller. Ron told me, "You take the kickoff no matter where it goes." He wasn't feeling well or something and I did. But I fumbled the ball. I still made a good run but I knew the Chargers had to make a cut and most likely it was going to be me.

Sid always told us we had to stay in our lane on kick returns. But Ron had told me to get it wherever it goes. Even though I fumbled it, I still returned it 34 yards.

But I had read in the papers that they were going to get rid of me. So we go back to the hotel the next day and Sid came to my room to cut me. He said, "Why didn't you stay in your lane and block for Waller?" I told him he didn't want to catch the ball.

Sid left the room and never came back. Instead I find out he cut Ron Waller instead of me.

I got a reprieve, but a lot of it had to do with returning that first kickoff 105 yards for a touchdown.

God had let me catch that kickoff that day and nobody could catch me. He gave me the gift to play football.

The only reason I got recognized and made the team was because of what I did on special teams. And the biggest thing I did was bringing that kickoff back 105 yards.

The Aftermath

When the Chargers beat the Boston Patriots for the 1963 AFL title—their only championship in franchise history—Paul Lowe was not the star he had become.

San Diego smoked the Patriots, 51–10, at Balboa Stadium. But Lowe, much like future Hall of Fame wide receiver Lance Alworth, was nothing but a ruse.

Instead of coach Sid Gillman leaning on his two aces, he pulled a fast one on the Patriots with fullback Keith Lincoln being the focal point. Lincoln didn't disappoint, collecting 349 yards and two touchdowns.

But Lowe was bummed.

"I was mad that they didn't give me the ball more," said Lowe, whose 12 rushes for 94 yards included a 58-yard touchdown. "Then again, you have to be a team player.

"But Sid had me and Lance running as decoys. The defenders would follow us on sweeps and such and that allowed Keith to get loose. The defense was spying on me and Lance.

"Sid put together a great game plan. He was a helluva coach."

And what a team that Chargers bunch was. Many—especially those in San Diego—believe the Chargers would have given the 1963 NFL champion Chicago Bears all they could handle.

"We had some good players," Lowe said. "And we played hard."

While Lowe recalls that game fondly, he also mentioned missing one of his good friends: Jack Kemp.

It wasn't difficult for Lowe, or anyone, to form a friendship with Jack Kemp. Lowe and Kemp had come south to San Diego from Los Angeles, but Kemp's Chargers days were behind him when the franchise won its biggest game.

"Not only was he a standout player but he was a helluva smart guy," Lowe said. "When we were on the bus he would be reading books about politics while I was reading the playbook to make the team."

Gillman tried to outsmart his counterparts in 1962. When Kemp broke his middle finger two games into the season, Gillman put Kemp through waivers to free up a roster spot.

Buffalo Bills coach Lou Saban got wind of Gillian's shenanigans and claimed Kemp for $100.

"He was our quarterback until Sid tried to do something funny," Lowe said, still steaming over Buffalo getting a star for nearly nothing. "Then he came back and kicked our butt for the 1964 [AFL] Championship."

But Lowe never let his love for Kemp waver. Lowe's kids would later babysit for the Kemp family. And when Kemp was Bob Dole's running mate for the 1996 presidential election, Lowe was a tireless worker to help his buddy become the vice president.

"I campaigned all up and down the West Coast for Jack," Lowe said. "Jack was really a beautiful person."

As a fan of Kemp's, Lowe had few peers. But Lowe wasn't so big on Gillman, as they often had heated discussions regarding playing time and contracts.

Once after a practice in sultry La Mesa, a San Diego suburb, Lowe tried an end-around—with a fan.

"We were working out there and it used to get hot," Lowe said, with a mischievous grin. "So one day I had taken a fan home from one of the meeting rooms, and it had to be Sid's fan.

"He came out where I was living and was mad as hell. He said, 'Where is my fan?' One of the guys I rode with must have told him—it might have been Jim Tolbert. But one of the guys snitched on me.

"So Sid says he is going to let me go and he did a couple of years later. I told him he didn't pay me enough to go buy one and that one was handy."

Same goes for the AFL–NFL merger, unless you were Lowe.

Lowe told Gillman in 1966 he wanted a salary of $50,000. Gillman declined, noting that the Cleveland Browns' Jim Brown made that much. Lowe countered that he was the Jim Brown of the AFL.

"We'll get back to you," Gillman said.

Lowe's patience didn't pay off, as he lost any leverage he may have had when the AFL and NFL merged.

"I waited for four, five weeks and then we merged with the NFL," Lowe said. "And that was that."

Chapter 2

RON MIX

Rams at Chargers—August 24, 1968

BIRTH DATE:	March 10, 1938
HOMETOWN:	Los Angeles, California
RESIDENCE:	Point Loma, California
JERSEY NO.:	74
POSITION:	Tackle
HEIGHT:	6-foot-4
WEIGHT:	255 pounds

The Run-Up

Ron Mix left the USC Trojans as one spent star.

"College football at that time was the most unbelievable grind you could ever imagine," said Mix, an All-American in 1959. "Current players wouldn't believe it.

There was no limit on the amount of time teams could keep you on the practice field. There was no limit of time spent in meetings. No limit to the amount of physical contact that could take place during practice.

"At the University of Southern California and probably every other major university in the country your practices were 2 ½ to 3 hours long and about four days a week it was full speed and hitting all the time.

"So if you didn't play a skilled position, you never had any fun. You just had the satisfaction of doing your job well."

While the Trojans' cry was "Fight On!" in the Los Angeles Memorial Coliseum, for Mix it was a chore to fight through it.

"We would leave the practice field and it wasn't enough that the practices were so long and tough," he said. "Afterward we would run wind sprints and leave practice just completely exhausted."

After his senior season, Mix caught the interest of the NFL's Baltimore Colts and the upstart AFL's Los Angeles Chargers.

The man who would become the second AFL player inducted into the Pro Football Hall of Fame was looking for a quick buck and an early exit from football.

"I just wanted to play football a couple of years and make enough money to buy a car and a house," Mix said. "College players had to play the entire game; you weren't either an offense or defensive player. It was just a grind and I assumed pro football would be that same way.

"But it wasn't. You only had to play on one side of the ball so some of the pleasure came back to the game. I fell in love with the game all over again and wanted to play as long as I could."

Now a professional, Mix weighed his options.

"I was the Colts' number one draft choice and they offered me a $1,000 bonus and a one-year contract at $7,500," Mix said. "And the Chargers offered a two-year guaranteed contract at $12,000 a year plus a $5,000 bonus.

"I told Colts owner Carroll Rosenbloom—in those days you didn't have agent—that I'd rather play for the Colts. If you would just give me a $2,000 bonus and a one-year contract at $10,000 that doesn't have to be guaranteed."

Rosenbloom then executed a block that would make Mix envious.

"Ron, that's like John Unitas money, and that would throw off our entire salary structure," Rosenbloom said. "Look, this new league is going to fold in a year anyway. We will see you back here next year and you will have a year of experience, which would be good for both of us."

Mix did move after his rookie year in 1960. But it was with the Chargers as they relocated to San Diego.

Rosenbloom was left wondering what might have been.

"I heard three or four years later that Carroll Rosenbloom had commented to someone that if he knew I was Jewish, he would have signed me," Mix said with a smile. "He said, 'We have a big Jewish population in Baltimore and he would have been popular.'"

The Game

By Ron Mix

I know the old-time San Diego fan base would like me to say the 1963 [AFL] Championship Game because the team, as a whole, came together and each individual played the finest game of their career. It was actually an amazing display of football greatness.

Coach [Sid] Gillman and his staff did a sensational job. We had a complete offensive explosion on the one side and the defense of that team was often overlooked.

Among those on defense were two of the greatest linemen to play the game in Ernie Ladd and Earl Faison. In my opinion each of them, had they not had injuries, would be in the Pro Football Hall of Fame. They played their position as well as anyone.

But being more shallow than that, to me the most significant game in my career was the second time our team played the Los Angeles Rams.

The first time they thumped us thoroughly [50–7]. And this is going to sound immodest but for the first time in my career, and for the only time, I conceded the defensive end got the better of me and that would be Deacon Jones.

It so concerned me that I told myself that is never going to happen again.

At that time Deacon was a great player, 6-foot-5, 275 pounds, and his greatest strength was really his quickness, far more than the fact [that] he was big and strong.

I played at 255 pounds, which was somewhat about the average of a tackle's weight in those days.

In the offseason, I increased my weightlifting training and gained 15 pounds.

I always studied the film and I figured [Jones] out. I determined that the best technique was not taking him on at the line of scrimmage.

[Offensive line coach] Joe Madro, he was the one who called me "The Intelligent Assassin" in part because I was going to law school at night. The assassin part was because unlike most tackles I was very aggressive at the line of scrimmage. But you can't do that with Deacon. You would have to have a variety of techniques and do it very quick. I would take a drop back and then when he makes his move, I would get into him and take him into the direction he is going.

I also determined when he was reaching out for his famous head slap, that the best thing is to become the assassin again by reaching out to him because his whole body is open and I would immediately thrust into his body.

And then I also decided cutting him now and then would also be effective.

The second game we beat the Rams [35–13], and everything I had thought about in using those techniques when I played against Deacon turned out to be true.

As a matter of fact one of my teammates at the University of Southern California was Monte Clark, an offensive tackle for the Cleveland Browns.

They played the Rams the following week after we had played them and Monte wrote to me and said that he had seen the game film and it was the best game he had ever seen anyone play against Deacon.

For me that was a very important game, to know that I could play against the greatest.

When [Jones] beat me the first time I felt that was the first time I had ever been beaten. It really shook me up.

Then we dominated them as much as they had dominated us in the first game.

The Aftermath

Ron Mix, civil rights leader?

Long after Mix retired, he's celebrated for being a shining example off the field, but perhaps for the same reason why he excelled in the game of his life—because he stood his ground when he believed in the success behind a plan.

The scene was the 1965 AFL All-Star Game in New Orleans, to be played in Tulane Stadium. The Crescent City was primed to put its best face forward as it longed to acquire a professional football franchise.

With the Civil Rights Act just being passed the previous year, some black players were hesitant about their reception in this Southern locale. But New Orleans politicians assured them the environment was safe and welcoming, inviting the players to bring their wives and children.

"All the players arrived in New Orleans and we checked into the hotel and we were given itineraries and told to get on the bus in the morning," Mix said. "We get on the bus and the coaches are taking the roll and everyone that is there says, 'Here.'

"They said, 'Bobby Bell.' No answer. They said, 'Earl Faison.' No answer. They said, 'Ernie Ladd.' No answer.

"The coaches said, 'Where is everybody?'"

The game's 21 black players were absent, considering their next move. Upon arriving in New Orleans, some were stranded at the airport for hours. They were denied entrances in restaurants and bars. They were the target of disgraceful language that would make even football players blush.

"One of the guys said, 'All the black guys are meeting. They are talking about boycotting the game because [of] the way they had been treated in New Orleans,'" Mix recalled.

While others paused, Mix sprung into action.

"I got off the bus and went to their meeting," he said. "I was the only white guy that got off the bus and I went to them and asked what happened?

"They told me they had a very hard time getting taxis. They went to restaurants and were turned away. They went to bars and one group of players was turned away by gunpoint. They said they were just not going to stay."

It was a tumultuous time in a shifting America and the fledgling AFL had a front-row seat to the sea change the nation was undergoing. New Orleans had promised no race-related problems, but truthfully, it was a city where segregation was still very real.

Mix, the future lawyer, reasoned with his black colleagues.

"What about staying and calling attention to all of this to the national media?" Mix said. "[Buffalo Bills fullback] Cookie Gilchrist was kind of moderating the meeting and he said, 'No, that [is] not enough. We have got to leave this place.'"

No sports league in America had ever boycotted a city over its treatment of blacks. This was a milestone event, not only for professional football, but for the nation as a whole.

The black players had a strong supporter in Mix.

"I said, 'OK I will go with you,'" Mix said. "Even though I was the only white guy that got off the bus, to the credit of the rest of the white athletes, I never heard one of them complain [about their missing teammates]."

The game was moved to Houston, but the reverberations from that day were lasting.

"Actually, that incident played a very important role in the desegregation history of America," Mix said. "At that time New Orleans wanted to get an NFL franchise and it then knew that wasn't going to happen unless it desegregated the city. So they passed legislation to desegregate the city.

"No longer could restaurants, bars, and other public places turn people away for race, religion, or any other reason that was being done at [the] time."

Slowly the white drinking fountains disappeared, as did blacks being denied services others enjoyed.

All because of a courageous group of black players, and a staunch backer in Mix.

"That game did desegregate the city," Mix said. "And I think it may have inspired black athletes to be more active in civil rights. Because the civil rights movement was just beginning to bloom.

"That was probably the first time black athletes, as a group, took a public stand."

Mix's contribution didn't go unnoticed.

"I know in later times, often when Cookie Gilchrist would be interviewed," Mix said, "when that subject was brought up, he expressed appreciation for the role I played."

Chapter 3

LANCE ALWORTH

Patriots at Chargers—January 5, 1964

BIRTH DATE:	August 3, 1940
HOMETOWN:	Houston, Texas
RESIDENCE:	Del Mar, California
JERSEY NO.:	19
POSITION:	Wide receiver
HEIGHT:	6-foot-0
WEIGHT:	184 pounds

The Run-Up

"Batting first and playing center field for the New York Yankees, Lance Alworth!"

Before Alworth became "Bambi" he had visions of patrolling an outfield once graced by the "Bambino."

"I got drafted by the Yankees and I almost signed with them in the summer of my senior year," Alworth said. "My dad said, 'No, you're going to college' and that was the end of that."

Alworth was a can't-miss all-around athlete at Brookhaven (Miss.) High School. After earning 15 letters, he was whistling "Dixie" about playing football for the University of Mississippi.

But before Alworth could produce a Rebel yell, a technicality got in the way.

"I had signed to go to Ole Miss and then I got married in high school," Alworth said. "At that time Ole Miss' football team had a rule that if you were married you couldn't get a scholarship. So it wanted to give me a baseball scholarship and said I could just come out for football."

But that scenario didn't pass the parental sniff test.

"The girl's parents and my parents said that was not the right thing to do," Alworth said. "So I went to the University of Arkansas."

Ole Miss's loss was Arkansas's gain. Alworth, a flanker, caught everything thrown his direction. As a punt returner, he paced the nation in yardage in 1960 and 1961. He also ran track. Eventually, he ran off to the NFL.

Alworth was drafted eighth overall by the San Francisco 49ers in 1962. He was also selected with the ninth pick that year in the AFL Draft by the Oakland Raiders.

The Raiders traded his rights to the Chargers and Alworth decided the free-wheeling AFL suited his style. The Chargers had a wide receivers coach in Al Davis, and the future Raiders owner, who was in his last year on the San Diego staff, was smitten with Alworth.

It was Davis who recruited Alworth, convincing him the Chargers, with offensive guru Sid Gillman at the controls, were preferable to the more stoic approach employed by the 49ers.

Davis would likely curse fate years later as Alworth developed into the AFL's first superstar. He would help the Chargers beat Davis's Raiders on many occasions, but the two remained close friends until Davis's death in 2011.

In fact, it was Davis who presented Alworth when he was inducted into the Pro Football Hall of Fame in 1978. Alworth was the first AFL player to be enshrined in Canton, Ohio.

Davis's involvement makes for a good tale. But it was Alworth landing on his tailbone that wrecked his rookie season in 1962.

It came about with Alworth playing the role of Charlie Brown, and teammate Keith Lincoln, that of Lucy.

"Keith and I were competitive in every way," Alworth said. "So we were practicing field goals and we were holding for each other. He kicked two or three good ones and so did I.

"So we go back to about 40 yards and he kicked his. Then when I went to kick mine, he pulled the ball away from me. I popped the heck out of my quad, tearing the muscle in my right thigh.

"We went to see the trainers and they said there was nothing wrong with me. But you could put your finger in the muscle and feel the hole in there. So I said, 'OK, I'll see if I can run a pattern on the outside. If I can make the catch, then I'm not hurt.'

"John [Hadl] threw it out to me and I took two steps and that was as far as I could go."

Alworth would become the only player named to the All-AFL and the NFL's 75th Anniversary teams.

The Game

By Lance Alworth

I loved them all. It's really hard to pinpoint one game back then. There were so many games that were exciting.

In all honesty, when looking back at it and when I'm asked by people which plays or which games I remember, it's when I dropped the ball or screwed up.

But that 1963 team, I remember the good times we had. It was just a great team; the fun we had together. It was the morale of everybody and how well we played together.

And it was the aspect of that AFL Championship Game that made it the most fun. It was because of the way we shocked them.

That was a great game and it was strictly designed for Keith Lincoln. It really was.

It was the way we attacked the Patriots; we had beat them 7–6 earlier in the season. That was a tough game and they were blitzing us a lot and [coach] Sid [Gillman] figured they were going to be doing the same thing.

So to counter that, he let the fullback, Lincoln, carry the ball a lot. Sid made it look like everyone else was going to get it and it ended up that Keith had a fabulous ball game.

We did a lot of misdirections and I can recall just a lot of traps up the middle. But we acted like we were threatening to throw it to the outside and the Patriots had to pay attention to us.

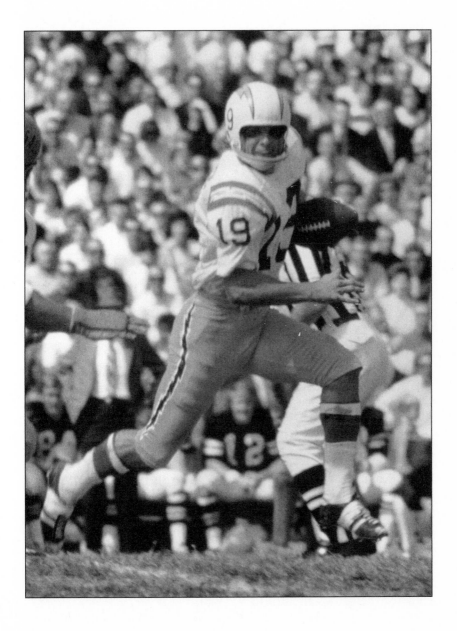

Sid split us out real wide and said to run down the field on every play and don't even look back. So we ran them off on every play and made them turn their backs to keep up with us. They ran with us on the outside.

They would follow you all the way and it was just as good as a block. All of a sudden, two defensive players are gone chasing us to the outside.

So Keith would go right up the middle or go right off tackle.

I think I caught four passes and one touchdown pass. And that touchdown came in the latter part of the ball game after we were so far ahead.

And our defense was a great defense to begin with. Our defensive backs, those guys were great cover guys and we had two tough safeties. And it was a great line with Earl Faison and Ernie Ladd— all those guys.

It wasn't just the great offense that we had. It was our defense, too. That's why that was the best football team I ever played on. We really had a good team, that '63 team. We beat the Patriots, 51–10.

And they never figured it out the whole ball game, as we kept going to Keith. He had 206 yards rushing—for a fullback! Keith was a great fullback and fast. And he had 123 yards receiving. He just had a fantastic ball game and honestly it was designed that way by Sid. That was the game plan and it really worked.

I remember everybody in the city was just so excited. In that day and age, football isn't what it was today. Football today has gotten so far beyond the image of what it had been. Now there is so much publicity and there is so much money involved. Now they see the games all around the world.

I wish we could have played the Chicago Bears after winning the AFL championship. They had won the NFL title and it was just the fact that we felt like we could challenge the Chicago Bears. We talked about it in the papers and I have no idea if they would take us up on it. But I do feel like it would have been a helluva ballgame. It sure would have been fun.

And I think us talking about it, and how good our team was, that was one of the things that helped make the Super Bowl happen.

The Aftermath

In the 1960s, San Diego was known for its sun and its star: the Chargers' Lance Alworth.

But in 1971, the sun remained while the star was sent packing to the Lone Star State.

"I was surprised," Alworth said, the shock still resonating in his voice all these years later. "I didn't think San Diego would trade me. I had no idea I was on the trading block and wasn't even thinking about it."

Fellow receiver Gary Garrison had become the focal point of the passing attack. Garrison led the Chargers with 44 catches and 12 touchdowns in 1970. Alworth had but 35 receptions for four scores and change was in the air.

The Chargers stumbled to the finish under coach Charlie Waller, winning but once in the final five weeks. After the 5–6–3 season, Waller was shown the exit.

That revolving door hit Alworth, too, and his next stop was Texas.

"I showed up at the airport in Dallas and there was nobody there to meet me," Alworth said. "Then I go see the coach

[Tom Landry] and he doesn't say 'Welcome to the team' or 'Glad you are here' or 'I'm happy we got you.' Nothing."

Alworth still can't erase the memory of Landry's Spartan office.

"There was nothing in it," Alworth said. "It was completely bare bones and he really doesn't even look up at me. Then he finally says we traded for you so you can block. He said if you will block we will win the Super Bowl and he turned around and walked out of the room without saying anything else."

Alworth, who had the sweetest hands in San Diego, was being asked to do grunt work with his sure-handed mitts? Surely Landry was joking, but the punch line was never delivered.

First Alworth absorbed the haymaker of being peddled by the Chargers. Then he was floored by the prospect of being an afterthought in the Cowboys' offense.

"One time during a ball game I was doing some turn-ins, where I would run 15-, 20-yard patterns and turn to the inside and come back to the ball," Alworth said. "I had run them so many times that I knew I could do them.

"So I said, 'Hey Coach, look for me with that turn-in and the quarterback can hit me for a touchdown.'"

Instead Landry stared right through Alworth. He may have been the feather in the Chargers' fedora, but Landry gave him a disapproving glare.

"If we're going to throw any touchdown passes it's going to be to No. 22, Bob Hayes," Landry said.

Alworth got the message.

"I never said another word," Alworth added.

Landry's demeanor had subtracted the drive from Alworth, something that's not easy to do.

"It just was not a pleasant time in my life," Alworth said. "It was the latter part of my career and it was difficult to work hard to stay in shape because I knew I was not going to get a shot. There wasn't a lot of incentive."

Alworth helped get that Super Bowl VI title for Landry, catching the game's first touchdown pass. One figures Alworth aced his blocking assignments, too.

"They wanted me to block and we won the Super Bowl," Alworth said. "So I guess he was right about that. But it was the most disappointing part of my career."

Chapter 4

LESLIE "SPEEDY" DUNCAN

Chiefs at Chargers—October 15, 1967

BIRTHDATE:	August 10, 1942
HOMETOWN:	Tuscaloosa, Alabama
RESIDENCE:	Spring Valley, California
JERSEY NO.:	45
POSITION:	Cornerback, kick returner
HEIGHT:	5-foot-10
WEIGHT:	180 pounds

The Run-Up

It's easy to see how Speedy Duncan, blessed with amazing speed, got his nickname. One doesn't score 26 touchdowns as a senior on an 11–0 prep football team in Tuscaloosa, Alabama, and not go unnoticed.

And by caddying at the Tuscaloosa Country Club, it seemed everyone knew, or knew of, Duncan.

But despite his resume and connections in town, Duncan couldn't play for the hometown team: The University of Alabama.

"Shoot, when we went by the school and they were practicing, all they would let us do was maybe peek under the fence," Duncan said. "But I wasn't going to be able to play there; no blacks did that back then. So I knew I was going to Jackson State."

Duncan, instead, became a star at the all-black college in the neighboring state of Mississippi. He was coached by Joe Gilliam, father of future Steelers quarterback Joe Gilliam Jr.

"I used to carry him around on my shoulders," Duncan said of the younger Gilliam. "Joe was good—good people."

Duncan proved how good he was as a shutdown cornerback by playing a certain wide receiver at Florida A&M to a standstill: Bob Hayes.

"I was matched against Bob Hayes and he was, as they say, the fastest man in the world," Duncan said. "And I said, 'I don't care who you are.' Maybe Bob Hayes could run off and leave me at 50 yards, but from zero to 50, I was quick as a cat and I could fly. It was fun battling him."

But a leg injury derailed Duncan's senior year. He planted with his right leg when coming up to make a tackle. His groin took the brunt of the shock and it took 40 stitches to repair it.

That torpedoed his chances of being snagged by the NFL or the AFL.

"I was predicted to be in one of the drafts and then I missed my last seven games of the season," he said. "Six weeks after surgery I was running full blast, but I got passed up in the draft."

Chargers scout Al LoCasale saw Duncan's potential. But when arriving at the Chargers' 1964 training camp in the north San Diego suburb of Escondido, Duncan did so as a free agent.

"We ran 40-yard dashes in training camp and I ran a 4.4," Duncan said. "Nobody before had run a 4.6. The coaches said, 'Run that again little fella because something ain't right.'"

The stopwatch didn't lie and Duncan backed up his quick times with bravado.

"I came here with 10 cents in my pocket and I would race anybody for a dime," he said. "When you're a free agent coming from Jackson State, well, I was trying to get the coaches' attention. You got to make them notice you. I was always a competitive guy and I didn't care who you are. I'll beat you, so let's do it."

Duncan had a long climb up the chart—he was with the fourth set of defensive backs.

"And during that time they had quotas [for black players] and only kept so many," he said. "But I told them, 'I ain't going nowhere.' I wasn't going to leave and I don't care what I have to do to make this club."

Duncan's dream took a haymaker during camp, after absorbing a helmet to his face. A broken cheekbone nearly broke his heart.

"When I got to the sidelines I couldn't even talk," he said. "But I got better and they put me on the taxi squad. Then I got a chance against Denver in an exhibition game and the first time

I touched the ball I laid it down in the end zone 66 yards away. I knew they weren't going to get rid of me then."

Duncan was right, which gave him the right to negotiate his first pro football contract. When asked his compensation for that first year, the man was quick with his reply: "$12,000!"

The Game

By Leslie "Speedy" Duncan

My favorite game is the one that I got out alive.

No really, my favorite game was against Kansas City, when we beat them, 45–31. I had a 100-yard pass interception, punt returns for 60-some yards, and returned a fumble 35 yards for a touchdown.

Earlier Chris Burford had run a quick out on me. I knew they would bring the play back and do that one more time.

They were right on the goal line and here it came again. I picked it and returned it for a 100-yard touchdown. After I caught it, I didn't see anything. I went straight down the sidelines untouched. I just thought to myself, *Don't you step out of bounds,* and I didn't.

Chris was tall, 6-foot-3, but he wasn't the fastest man in the world. And you didn't have a lot of people playing bump-and-run back then and I did. Because I always knew I could control you up on top.

When he ran his route, I let him get into me and I knew he was going to do the same route. As he was pushing off and he got his body away from me, I went the same way, where I wanted him to go. I came right off him and I was right there when the pass came. I took the ball right off his hands.

When you're a cornerback, you turn and instincts tell you he is going to do certain things so he can get his big body into me. Then when he pushed off, I went with him and just kept going. He couldn't get the ball away from me.

You have to remember playing defensive back wasn't the only thing I did. I had to return punts and kickoffs and do the special-teams coverages. I did everything and they never wanted to pay us [any] money.

I tell you what. You get yourself in shape back then when you run all day, that's for sure.

When the Chiefs got down close to the goal line, I knew they were going to come back to that route with Chris and I got them. And when I caught it, I was running down my sideline and I didn't care what anyone else was doing, I was gone. I was going to the house.

I knew they weren't going to catch me; they didn't even try. I could bring it back.

But most of the time I would be so tired from playing defense, then I had to drop back on fourth down for punts. When they send the receivers deep on you a couple of times, whether they catch the ball or not, you've got to go. If I would've just returned punts and kicks, I would have been a monster.

Remember the Chiefs had a pretty good team. Otis Taylor was their flanker. But I was the right corner, so I would cover whoever came over to my side. Sometimes [Taylor and Buford] would come to my side and I would have to play over the top and the safety would have to come over to the right side.

They were really our rivals, being in the same conference, and we used to beat the bark off of them.

Yep, 45–31. All I know is if you get the opportunity, you don't blow the opportunity. You got to make sure you get it.

The Aftermath

Speedy Duncan nearly did everything for the Chargers. What he couldn't do was make coach and general manager Sid Gillman appreciate him. The two had sparred before over issues and then Gillman's contract negotiations in 1971 with Duncan hit a speed bump.

"I just got tired with Sid Gillman and I wasn't talking to him anymore," Duncan said. "You can make a ballplayer not want to play for you if you get beat down all the time. I was really, really angry with the Chargers.

"I'd be leaving practice and be so mad and he would say, 'Little fella, come talk to me' and I would just keep on walking. I know that was his job to get me signed for as little as he could but they don't understand what you got to go through. They were beating me up returning punts, kickoffs, playing right cornerback, and covering kicks and field goals."

His dream of playing for the Chargers turned into a nightmare. Once so eager not to leave, Duncan requested a trade through owner Gene Klein.

"And boy did they trade me—as far away as they could," Duncan said.

He landed with the Washington Redskins where, of course, the future was now.

"I got to play for [coach] George Allen," Duncan said.

He also got to meet future President Ronald Reagan. The two played catch at a Washington, D.C., function.

"I remembered him in *Knute Rockne All American,* when he returned punts, like me," Duncan said with pride. "I told him I used to watch him in those old Westerns and that he was my governor when I was in California."

Duncan would later return to the Golden State, teaching health and physical education for more than 20 years.

"I didn't expect to play pro ball so I got my [degree] at Jackson State," he said. "I would have been up a creek without that."

If so, and in knowing Duncan, it would have been a fast-moving body of water.

Chapter 5

DOUG WILKERSON

Raiders at Chargers—September 10, 1978

BIRTH DATE:	March 27, 1947
HOMETOWN:	Fayetteville, North Carolina
RESIDENCE:	Rancho Santa Fe, California
JERSEY NO.:	63
POSITION:	Guard
HEIGHT:	6-foot-3
WEIGHT:	253 pounds

The Run-Up

Doug Wilkerson's skills at E. E. Smith High School in his native Fayetteville, North Carolina got the attention of many schools. He was a star on both sides of the line, opening holes for his ball-carriers and closing them for rival ones.

"I pretty much played all along the lines," he said.

He did so by displaying strength and technique. But what separated Wilkerson from others were his feet—he could run off them and quickly. Wilkerson was once clocked in 9.8 seconds while conquering the 100-yard dash.

But what the schools racing against each other to recruit Wilkerson couldn't trump was the love of his family. While Michigan State and Minnesota, among others, were intrigued by Wilkerson, his mind was made up. There was little doubt he would stick close to home, and that meant enrolling at North Carolina Central.

"There were a lot of guys interested in North Carolina Central from my high school," Wilkerson said. "And it was only 60 miles away, so my mom and dad could come up and watch me."

What they saw was a future NFL Pro Bowler being shaped. Wilkerson was a three-time all-conference player and twice was named an NAIA All-American. When the 1970 draft rolled around, it wasn't long until Wilkerson's name rolled off the Houston Oilers' tongue.

Wilkerson was selected 14th overall, the highest draft pick ever for a player hailing from North Carolina Central.

When he got to Houston, there was a bit of a problem: where to plop the impressive Wilkerson?

"I could basically pretty much play on either side of the ball," Wilkerson said. "But the coaches, they figured it out in my rookie year that I would go to the offensive side of the ball."

Settled on the field, Wilkerson saw action in nine games. But soon he would be in motion off of it, when he was traded to San Diego.

After one year with the Oilers, California was the place for Wilkerson to go next. Houston peddled Wilkerson to the Chargers to get tight end Willie Frazier back. In 1964–65, Frazier had been a standout with the Oilers, making the AFL All-Star team in '65.

"You just go ahead and keep moving," Wilkerson said about his life journey, which pointed him west. "Not only did we make our home in San Diego, but I got to play for Sid Gillman and that group. Their reputation had preceded them. Sid was a great innovator on offense and you knew of guys like Ron Mix and other players that had been there."

Wilkerson was comfortable in San Diego, taking up residence on an offensive line that was the backbone of Don Coryell's high-flying offenses.

Wilkinson's interior blocking prowess led to his inclusion in the Chargers Hall of Fame. He was also named to the team's 50th and 40th anniversary squads.

But save a trade after one year in Texas, Wilkerson would have never experienced playing for two of the Chargers' most legendary coaches: Gillman and Coryell.

The Game

By Doug Wilkerson

We had some excellent and very, very good players and the guys enjoyed playing as a team. That is what I remember—how we enjoyed playing with each other and being around one another. Those are the kinds of things you don't forget.

But I go back to one of the games we lost to the Raiders on the Holy Roller play. I think of that game and the losses to Oakland and Cincinnati in the playoffs. Those three games, which were losses, stick with me. That, and then the overtime playoff game in Miami that we were fortunate to win. Then we got to Cincinnati and, well, it didn't work out.

In the Holy Roller game we are leading in that ball game. And they ended up winning the game on that play.

It was always something when you played the Raiders. You knew you had to give your best all the time and reach down and find anything or use anything you could because [you've] got to win the game. They had one of the dominating teams that played during that era. They were like the Pittsburgh Steelers, in that class where they were always competing for the Super Bowl.

The Raiders would normally use a 3–4 defense. They had John Matuszak at end and Otis Sistrunk inside. Just great players. And one of the outside linebackers was Ted Hendricks. He could drop back in coverage and play that well, too.

The secondary had Lester Hayes; I mean it was just a very formidable team.

And they always tried to keep things going, if you know what I mean. They played on the edge. They were a good football team and they came to play. You knew you better bring your lunch pail because it was not going to be easy.

But we had Dan Fouts and he was a very, very special guy. He came to work every time we played. He expected you to do the same, because that was what he was going to be doing.

It was his leadership and definitely the fire that he played with. You always looked forward to playing with Dan because he was such a great competitor.

On the Holy Roller play the defense was on the field, so we were on the sidelines. You look back on it now and it was unfortunate what happened. They got a break when the quarterback, [Ken] Stabler, lost the ball. Somehow it made its way up the field and became a touchdown.

It was a disappointment because you see it happen and you saw how it was advanced and then that was the end of the game. It really just hit you because at that point, it ended the game.

The way they advanced the ball, well, it worked out for them—unfortunately. The officiating is much better now than then. Now they would have a chance to review it and when they saw how they advanced it, it would have been very difficult for them to score that way.

The Raiders had already won a Super Bowl at that point. So it was just one of those kinds of things. We were at a turning point with our franchise and starting to move forward.

We had Dan, John Jefferson, Ed White, Charlie Joiner, Billy Shields, [and] Russ Washington on offense.

On defense we had Fred Dean, Louie Kelcher—I mean that was a fantastic team.

And what was special about that game, and that time, was how great the fans were. You appreciated it as a player; it was such a good era. Plus we were one of the most electrifying and entertaining teams.

The Aftermath

The sting lingers to this day and that's how bad the Air Coryell Chargers wanted to go to the Super Bowl.

There was nothing quite like that thrilling brand of Chargers football that Wilkerson was part of in the late 1970s and early 1980s. No one scored more points, or threw for more yards, than those explosive teams. And they did so in a fashion that was hard to ignore.

"I want them to have to defend every inch of the field," Coryell once said.

So with Coryell spreading out his receivers and giving quarterback Dan Fouts the equivalent of a green light, fall Sundays in San Diego were a happening as much as they were about two teams playing football.

But that offense doesn't click with a chink in the offensive line. Wilkerson was part of that group, but there's still a part of him that can't shake regret.

"We couldn't get it done," Wilkerson said.

Nope, the Super Bowl was for other teams and Wilkerson said that still bugs him to this day. It's also among the reasons Coryell, one of the NFL's true innovators, remains on the outside of the Pro Football Hall of Fame. Coryell's teams, of which Wilkerson was an integral part, never reached a game with Roman numerals.

In 1979, Wilkerson's Chargers embarrassed both the Los Angeles Rams (40–16) and the Pittsburgh Steelers (35–7) during the regular season. Those teams were the featured attractions in Super Bowl XIV, while the Chargers could only watch the game from home.

That year the Chargers were eliminated in the divisional playoffs by Wilkerson's old team, the Oilers.

But Wilkerson said losing to his first team didn't match the bummer following the 1981 regular season. In consecutive playoff weeks, the Chargers absorbed both the elation and heartache that only postseason football offers.

"We go down to Miami and win that one in overtime in 90-degree heat," Wilkerson said. "Then we go to Cincinnati and we just couldn't get it done."

The Chargers' high-octane offense wasn't done in so much by the Bengals' defense as it was by Cincinnati's dumbfounding weather.

The frozen thermometer, when shook from its slumber, showed 9 degrees below zero. When including the blustery wind coming off the Ohio River, it was 59 below.

"It was extremely cold," Wilkerson said. "You couldn't feel your extremities. When you look back on it, it was just very unique.

"You really didn't understand how cold it was until you got out on the field. You prepare for it, and those kinds of things, but it actually hit you that Sunday morning."

The Bengals would prevail, 27–7, as Fouts was restricted to just 185 passing yards. But while recognizing how difficult the playing conditions were and the misery the loss brought, Wilkerson tips his hat to the Bengals.

"They were a very good football team," he said. "Whether the weather kept us from the Super Bowl, I can't say that. But when you get that close and you don't get it done, well, that's something that just stays with you.

"But we have no excuses; they were playing on the same field. They just outplayed us and we didn't finish the task at hand."

Chapter 6

CHARLIE
JOINER

Chargers at 49ers—December 11, 1982

BIRTH DATE:	October 14, 1947
HOMETOWN:	Many, Louisiana
RESIDENCE:	San Diego, California
JERSEY NO.:	18
POSITION:	Wide receiver
HEIGHT:	5-foot-11
WEIGHT:	188 pounds

The Run-Up

Charlie Joiner became Charlie Joiner because he became a Bengal before becoming a Bolt.

Joiner, a star at Grambling University, was drafted in 1969 by the AFL's Houston Oilers as a defensive back. It was a curious start to a Pro Football Hall of Fame career as a wide receiver, which included an eleven-year stint with the San Diego Chargers.

The Oilers had a valuable commodity in Joiner until 1972 but they didn't know it. His four years were mixed, as Houston couldn't decide which side of the ball for him to play.

He had just 82 receptions, although injuries also derailed his progress.

But his stellar career got on track with his introduction to Bill Walsh after being traded to the Cincinnati Bengals. His new team saw Joiner as a pass-catcher and he was ecstatic to connect with Walsh, its innovative offensive coordinator.

"He was just a fantastic person, a great guy," Joiner said. "It was Bill, and the other coaches, well they taught you how to play professional football, see what I mean?"

With the Bengals, Joiner not only met Walsh but embraced his West Coast offense. It was a scheme built around short passes replacing runs; multiple routes for receivers to get free.

Not only was Joiner under Walsh's supervision, but also a no-nonsense head coach in Paul Brown.

"They taught us how to prepare and be professional, really," Joiner said.

Those lessons began the first time Joiner was supposed to be at just a certain spot at just a certain time.

"Right away, the minute I stepped in the [team] room, it was instantly different," Joiner said. "There was a chair in the room with your name on it. And if the meeting was to start at nine o'clock, you couldn't just be in the room at nine o'clock; you had to be in your chair. If you were not in your chair, you were late.

"Paul Brown would say, 'Mr. Joiner you're late. Your chair is up there in front.' So I went up and got in my chair."

That was the drill in the first meeting and every other one, Joiner said.

"It was like that every day. He ran the organization in a way that everything was totally professional. It was just a different atmosphere, with Paul Brown, than it was in Houston," Joiner said.

Joiner had no problem with the discipline. He expected an equal dose when heading for his first powwow with Walsh.

"The receivers and the quarterbacks, they met together," Joiner said. "I go in and Bill Walsh is telling a funny joke. He was funny as hell. But then he got down to business. He said, 'It's going to be like this or like that.' But he was always encouraging and experimenting. He would change plays if they had to be changed."

Walsh's assessment of Joiner never wavered. He once said Joiner was "the most intelligent, the smartest, the most calculating receiver the game has ever known."

Joiner was a full-time receiver after taking his licks in the Oilers' secondary. He broke his arm trying to tackle the Denver Broncos' Floyd Little his rookie year.

"It was a double-compound fracture," Joiner said. "I thought my career was ended."

The following year, Joiner broke his other arm in training camp.

But he was finally healthy and out of Houston midway through the 1972 season when peddled to the Bengals.

Joiner had hoped he ditched the injury bug as well.

"Then I break my collarbone on the first play with Cincinnati in our first game, against the Browns," Joiner said. "I went up and caught the ball and came down the wrong way and broke my collarbone. I'm thinking, *Damn, maybe this game is not for me,* and it was time to do something else.'

"But Paul Brown said, 'Hey that's going to heal and you'll be ready.'"

Brown's words were gospel to Joiner.

He became known for his sure hands and durability, missing just one game in his final 13 seasons.

"I barely got a headache," Joiner said.

The Game

By Charlie Joiner

Playoff games are the important games of any franchise. But for me the most gratifying game I ever played in wasn't a playoff game.

For me it was that game against San Francisco, [Dan] Fouts vs. [Joe] Montana, and us winning that game 41–37.

That was big, big, big.

It was big because we beat [49ers coach] Bill Walsh. Bill was my coach at Cincinnati and any time you could beat Bill, it was something.

Now, he rebounded and won some more Super Bowls, don't get me wrong. But just to beat him, his philosophy and his coaches. That was just one of those games where everything came together.

It was one of the best games we ever played. It was just a great game, especially for Dan Fouts and Wes Chandler. It was unbelievable how Dan was throwing it and Wes was catching it.

And Joe Montana was playing.

I knew Montana was a great football player. And I knew the way Bill Walsh coached because I was with him in Cincinnati. I knew the way he would coach Montana once he got a hold of him.

That game proved to me that Joe was a great fit for the West Coast offense that Bill ran. Joe had that quick release and he could make the reads and if there was no one open he could throw it out to the running back. He made it look so easy. His reads didn't take him to the other side of the field. He would look to the right and if there was nothing there, his read would take him to that receiver over the middle. Then if nothing was there, he would throw it out in the flat. His delivery was quicker that day, he was more confident in his play.

His play and that offense mimicked what we were doing with [Chargers coach Don] Coryell. That's why we couldn't wait until Coryell took over [in 1978].

The West Coast offense and what Coryell was doing was almost the same thing. If you were the quarterback, [almost] nothing would take him over to the opposite side of the field. There weren't a lot of times his reads would take him to the other side to make him throw across his body.

Most everything was to the right. That was where the initial read would go and the quarterback would deliver it there. You were overloaded on that side of the field and most of the coverages were man-to-man back then.

But that game was something when you just think of the players on the field. They had Jerry Rice, Joe Montana, and

Dwight Clark. We had Fouts, Winslow, Chandler. And [offensive linemen] Ed White and Doug "Moosie" Wilkerson were there. Man, that sounds like a Pro Bowl.

And on defense the 49ers had Fred Dean and we had Gary Johnson.

To beat Walsh really meant something; it was special. That was basically a playoff game. In fact you aren't going to find anything better, even in a playoff game, than those two teams that matched up on that day.

A big reason why it was special for me was watching Wes Chandler. What a great day he had [seven receptions for 125 yards and three touchdowns] catching the ball.

He just kept making outstanding catches in that game. He would make them behind his head, over his shoulders—you name it. He made all the catches and I just remember what a game it was for Wes and Dan.

Wes was such a great athlete. I think athletically, he was just as good as anybody in the league. And athletically, he's just as good as anyone right now. You look at any receiver in the league right now, and Wes was just as good as they are.

The guy was so good. He could play any skill position or really anywhere on the field. He could play quarterback, running back, all those things. We knew what he could do as a wide receiver but he could have played tight end, too. Well, maybe that blocking would have got to him but he could play almost any position equally well.

He also had a great determination about him. Sometimes it didn't show, but he was a determined, determined guy. Especially when the game was big, like that one was.

Plus, man, he was some kind of a leader. He was vocal, now, and sometimes he could [tick] some people off. He didn't hold anything back. I think it got to people and that's just the way he laid it out.

He might have [ticked] you off but that got you up for the game. That is what leaders are supposed to do. That was his way to be a leader and he was a leader in that game against San Francisco.

Wes and Kellen [Winslow], they led in their own way.

Now Fouts, he was a demanding leader. He expected you to play at the same level he was going to play at. And really Wes, in some ways, was the same way as Dan. He talked the talk and he also walked the walk. He had all the leadership qualities anyone needs.

In that game, Chandler was a motivational kind of leader. He would tell you, "You need to get it together."

But that day meant so much because we beat Bill.

The Aftermath

The smooth-running Charlie Joiner was as quiet out of his routes as he was in the locker room.

Looking for a loud voice among the din of a noisy bunch of football players? Don't expect Joiner's voice to rise above others.

"I was not very vocal," Joiner said, of course, softly.

There were some hard choices for one of the all-time Chargers greats when he retired after the 1986 season, the last player from the AFL era to do so.

When stepping aside at age thirty-nine, Joiner did so with some impressive numbers, all then NFL records: most receptions (750), receiving yards (12,146), and games played (239) by a wide receiver.

So Joiner figured, he would turn to other figures.

"I had a degree in accounting and passed the CPA exam," Joiner said. "I was going to start in that business on the ground floor."

Instead he went upstairs, up to the coaches' offices, once he was convinced to do so by Chargers coach Al Saunders.

"I just didn't think I was coaching material," said Joiner, one of four Chargers to have his number retired. "But it worked out."

Joiner drew raves for lasting 18 years as a pro football player. Even he's amazed he went that long as a coach, plus eight more seasons.

In addition to two stints with the Chargers, Joiner coached with the Buffalo Bills and Kansas City Chiefs.

That's 44 years in the AFL and NFL for someone thinking his career was over when he broke his arm his rookie year.

Being a coach wasn't a snap for Joiner, but it was a role he grew into. He did so by being himself.

"I just tried to teach them the best I can and to prepare the players so the guy could play at his full ability." he said. "I think the job is a little easier if you keep it simple for them.

"Teach them the methods that they can really understand. Know the guy and teach it at his level."

One lesson fits all? Not exactly, Joiner stressed.

"When we would sign a guy, I would see what he understands and find out what made him tick," Joiner said. "You wouldn't coach some guy the way you would coach Kellen Winslow.

"What made them study harder and play their best? Each player was different. You couldn't have one general speech for everybody. You needed to use the right words to get the very best out of them."

But don't superstars often make subpar coaches?

Joiner didn't buy that argument then or now.

"I didn't believe that," Joiner said. "When I started coaching, [ex-Oakland Raiders great] Fred Biletnikoff was coaching. [Former Miami Dolphins star] Paul Warfield was doing it. You can't tell me they aren't great receivers; those guys were better receivers than I was. So if they were successful, I [didn't see] why I couldn't do it."

Joiner nearly did it all in pro football for almost five decades. That comes through loud and clear.

Chapter 7

DAN FOUTS

Chargers at 49ers—December 11, 1982

BIRTH DATE:	June 10, 1951
HOMETOWN:	San Francisco, California
RESIDENCE:	Sisters, Oregon
JERSEY NO.:	14
POSITION:	Quarterback
HEIGHT:	6-foot-3
WEIGHT:	204 pounds

The Run-Up

Dan Fouts is clear about how he got to Canton, Ohio.

"Without Don Coryell," Fouts said, "I wouldn't be in the Pro Football Hall of Fame."

Among Fouts's biggest disappointments is that Coryell has yet to join him there. Fouts freely talks of the impact Coryell had, not only with the Chargers' gunslinger quarterback, but throughout the game of pro football.

"Look at nearly every game on Sunday and you can see Don's influence," Fouts said. "And he was very influential in my development."

Fouts, as usual, has a point.

In his first five years with the Chargers, Fouts never threw for more than 14 touchdowns in a season.

Then when Coryell replaced Tommy Prothro after the Chargers started 1978 by dropping three of their first four games, few benefited as much as Fouts did.

Fouts finished with 24 scoring passes in Coryell's abbreviated first season, a figure he matched the following year. Then in 1980–81, the Air Coryell salad days, Fouts heaved a total of 63 touchdown passes.

"It was so creative," Fouts said of Coryell's approach. "It was like every Wednesday when he put the game plan in, it would be different. And we would have the knowledge that it would be successful. He wasn't doing stuff different [just] to be doing it. He did it so we could win.

"You would move the ball and it was really fun. On those Wednesdays I remember going out to practice so anxious, because it was just the start of us having a really good Sunday."

In 1979 the Chargers started a three-year run of winning the AFC West division and that included two trips to the AFC Championship Game. That the Chargers fell short in both their shots at a Super Bowl is among the reasons Coryell is excluded from the Hall of Fame.

But there was little doubt in Fouts's mind regarding his presenter when he was immortalized in Ohio.

Coach Coryell, the floor is yours.

"To many people Dan is a legend and the fans remember him I know as an inspirational leader and, of course, as a fearless competitor. He was a tall, feisty, bearded quarterback who had fire in his eyes and fans remember, of course, the way he walked to the line of scrimmage, the way he looked over the defense, and the way he called the signals.

"His opponents remember him because of his quick drop and the way he set and threw the ball without hesitation. He could see the whole field and find the receiver quickly. Dan would stay in the pocket to the last second and take a hit without flinching."

With Fouts as the pilot of Air Coryell's high-flying approach, he had ample targets in Charlie Joiner, Kellen Winslow, John Jefferson, and Wes Chandler. But the bearded ace doesn't hesitate in giving credit to Coryell.

"It was his numbering system of the passing game," Fouts said. "It was so simple and easy to learn that you could teach it to second-graders. And Don could teach it to his second-graders and beat your second-graders. Or take your second-graders and beat his with it."

Second to none was Fouts. But first things first, and that's Fouts reminding everyone that Coryell was a big reason for his success.

The Game

By Dan Fouts

I would have to say the first game that probably comes to mind is the shootout with Joe Montana in San Francisco.

For me it was significant because it was the first regular-season game for me in San Francisco. And it was the first and only one against Montana.

I remember it was the 1982 strike season. We played them on a Saturday afternoon and it was the national game of the week. And what I recall is there was no wind at Candlestick. It was calm, it was beautiful, and we had a great game.

I'm not sure who got the lead first, but I know it went back and forth.

Wes Chandler was out of his mind that day and caught three touchdowns. He was so great.

And Charlie [Joiner] was Charlie and Chuck [Muncie] was Chuck. It was all good.

We had to go down and score toward the end. I hit Muncie with a little swing pass and that was the game-winner. Just as I was throwing it, I got hit by Fred Dean in the back. It was a little play-action play and Chuck was isolated on a linebacker. Chuck beat him to the corner of the end zone.

Montana, though, still had some time left. But Woodrow Lowe picked off his pass at the end and that was pretty good for us.

I think Montana was knocked out of the game for a while after he got blasted pretty good. But the final was 41–37 so it wasn't like he didn't do his part during the other parts of the game that he was in there.

But to beat Bill Walsh, my former assistant coach in San Diego. And his assistant George Seifert, who recruited me to go to Oregon; he was our defensive backs coach at Oregon. It was always fun to go against your mentors.

And Montana was perfect for the style of offense Bill ran. He was such a smooth athlete and a real quiet competitor.

It was his quick reads, the agility in the pocket, the smarts. You got to be able to read the defense quickly and get rid of it and move if you have to because it is a short-drop passing game. He was just real smooth.

What was ironic about it after we beat the 49ers was [that] the following game was [against the Bengals] on *Monday Night Football*. We beat Cincinnati by putting 50 points on them.

Both those teams were in the Super Bowl the previous year and we beat them.

But for me it was special going back to San Francisco, obviously.

Having grown up in the city and then having been a 49ers ball boy when my dad was the voice of the 49ers, it was all surreal. I had played preseason games in Candlestick, but that was like for one or two series. This time I was out there knowing that half the people in the stands were rooting against me and the others were pulling for me, quietly. It was unbelievable.

One of the moments I remember is after the game I did an interview with Montana on the field.

From that point, it's a long walk to the locker room. While I was walking off the field I see a police officer in uniform and he came up to me and said, "Hello." It was a classmate of mine from grammar school and high school and I reached around him and put my arm around him while I was walking off the field.

When I did that, I felt his bulletproof vest. I said, "Are you kidding me?"

He told me it was his American Express card. You know, he never leaves home without it.

But just the thought of that made me realize what his job was. And that mine seemed simple.

The Aftermath

Fouts had a rocket for an arm. But there was little turbo in his giddy-up, which meant he often got flattened when buying an extra second to deliver another pinpoint pass.

One day after getting smoked, his eyes cleared and drifted from the pass-rusher's jersey toward the press box.

"I was sitting there on my backside after a second-and-long had become third-and-longer," Fouts said. "I look up at [the] broadcasting booth and see Merlin Olsen up there and I thought, *That looks like a good gig up there.*"

Fouts's keen sense of timing wasn't restricted to between the sidelines. After he retired following the 1987 season, he turned to calling games instead of calling out winning cadences.

That transition isn't surprising, considering Fouts's father, Bob, was an all-everything broadcaster in San Francisco.

"Obviously my dad was a huge influence," said the legendary quarterback of his legendary father. "There were many times I would keep stats for him in the booth during [a] 49ers game.

"But he didn't just do the 49ers. He was the voice of [the] University of San Francisco Dons when it won back-to-back national titles with Bill Russell. Then when the Warriors came he did those games with Bill King. He did California and Stanford basketball, all that stuff in the Bay Area. And I got to go to all of it."

Few, though, were all in with Fouts being a media member. He had been quite salty to cover when playing for the Chargers—especially after losses.

"I admit my shortcomings," he said, of his bone-chilling stare he would give reporters asking inane questions. "I know I [ticked] a lot of guys off.

"But I was mad at myself because when that happened we usually lost. And it's the quarterback's fault usually that you lost and then you had to speak about it.

"Yeah, I was testy. There was no question. But it's very unnatural to discuss a ball game, win or lose, right after it, but especially after you lose. It's tough to do. And you couldn't throw people under the bus or anything like that."

Fouts has gotten plenty of mileage from his second profession. He's advanced from being a San Francisco sports anchor to calling college games to being part of the *Monday Night Football* crew to working on CBS TV and Westwood One radio.

Fouts has shared the microphone with some of the industry's giants: Dick Enberg, Keith Jackson, Al Michaels, Verne Lundquist, Brent Musburger, and the list goes on.

Analyzing the game doesn't match playing it, but there are some similarities, Fouts said.

"You get some of the same satisfaction because it is live and you have to prepare," he said. "I tell my kids it's like taking an oral test for three-and-a-half hours every Sunday. But you don't have one teacher, you have millions of teachers that are critiquing you. I always keep that in mind when I am doing my preparation.

"Then there's the teamwork that is involved that I really enjoy. There's the producer, the director, the statistician, the spotter . . . there are hundreds of people that are behind the scenes and you work with the same people every week. So it really is like a team."

Once the red light flickers, Fouts again shines as the captain.

"I really enjoy it," he said. "I'm really lucky I've been able to stick around this long."

Chapter 8

HANK BAUER

Chargers at Seahawks—November 27, 1977

BIRTH DATE:	July 15, 1954
HOMETOWN:	Scottsbluff, Nebraska
RESIDENCE:	Poway, California
JERSEY NO.:	37
POSITION:	Running back
HEIGHT:	5-foot-10
WEIGHT:	200 pounds

The Run-Up

Hank Bauer was the classic overachiever while playing at Cal Lutheran College in Thousand Oaks, California.

It just happened that's where the Dallas Cowboys held their training camp. After graduating from Cal Lutheran, Bauer was invited to the 1976 Cowboys camp as an undrafted rookie.

He lasted three weeks.

"And I thought I was killing it," Bauer said with a laugh. "One day I'm with the Cowboys and the next day I'm sleeping in my brother's garage in nearby Oxnard. But I knew I was good enough to play in the NFL."

It was hardly a confidence-building experience for a player that would be named to the Chargers' 50th and 40th anniversary teams, someone who would become a team captain despite being mostly a special-teams player, someone who once had a game where he scored three touchdowns on four carries, while rushing for a total of 1 yard.

Bauer is certain that, without the heartache of getting cut and spending a year teaching in high school, he wouldn't have accomplished what he did.

"That was a great blessing for me to go to a small school and not get drafted," Bauer said. "I made it the hard way. It made me appreciate and realize it's really the relationships and experiences that count. All that other stuff, it's not real."

The make-believe NFL world makes some miss the big picture, Bauer said.

"When you get older and you start going into the fourth quarter of your life, people realize that," he said. "Unfortunately not enough people see it early enough."

Bauer couldn't focus in a 1977 preseason game against the Los Angeles Rams. Trying to impress the Chargers that he had the goods, what Bauer didn't have was his wits.

On the game's kickoff, Bauer charged down the field like a madman. But instead of making the tackle, he was blindsided by L.A.'s Tom Mack when the Rams ran a reverse.

Once Bauer gathered himself, he headed for the sideline—the Rams' sideline. One of their players pushed him back toward the field and he ended up wandering around the end zone until a Charger rescued his woozy teammate.

Despite the hit, Bauer later returned to the game.

Bauer made the team and made his mark his rookie season as a special-teams dynamo. Then in 1978–79, he saw additional playing time in the backfield as a short-yardage specialist.

But the Chargers acquired powerful running back Chuck Muncie in 1980. The following year James Brooks, another running back, was the team's top pick in the draft.

Bauer was a bit quirky, but he wasn't stupid. He could decipher the tea leaves, which said his days carting the football were numbered.

So he focused on special teams, with a zeal few have seen before or since.

"I relished it," he said. "It was a blue-collar job. If I left a legacy at all, it was to legitimize special teams."

The Game

By Hank Bauer

We were in Seattle and I was going to be playing a little on offense. Before that it was all special teams, which was fine, too. I was just trying to do whatever they wanted me to do and I was loving every

minute of it. I was an undrafted rookie and nobody knew me. I was at the bottom of the roster.

My dad had a history of heart issues and he was in the hospital, north of Sacramento. He had gone into the hospital for some tests, which was what my family told me. They didn't want me to worry about him.

Now remember there was no Internet or access to the games. You had to be on the game of the week, or otherwise, your family wasn't going to see you play. But the Seattle game was a rare one because we were on TV. This was going to be the first time my dad saw me play on TV.

So I call the hospital—on a landline—and tell him I'm going to do something really good for you.

What I didn't know was my dad was in the Intensive Care Unit.

I heard he had watched the game and saw me on a couple of plays and on special teams. I couldn't wait to get home on Sunday night after the game and call him.

On the team flight, I ate exactly what everybody else did. I was pumped up. I was healthy.

I was fine when I got into my 1968 VW that was five different colors and had a hole in the floorboard; I was making $20,000 a year. I rushed to my apartment, which I was renting on a month-to-month basis, and I can remember that I was just so excited to call him. So I call the hospital.

I reached the hospital switchboard at 9:20 that night and the nurses say, yeah, your dad saw the game and he is really excited. But we can't let you to talk to him because it's after nine, so on and so forth.

I thought *OK*, and I went to bed. Then in the middle of the night I get violently ill. I mean it was bad. I was throwing up and I ended up lying in the bathroom the whole night.

I get down to the stadium early the next day because I thought I got food poisoning. But the trainers said that wasn't the problem. And that everyone else on the team had eaten the same thing and they didn't get sick, so it couldn't have been that.

Soon I find out that my dad passed away during the night, at the same time that I started to get sick. That's crazy, right?

Big Hank, my dad, had died at the same time I got so violently ill after the game of my life because he was watching me play on TV for the very first time.

The Aftermath

Bauer earned his first game ball following the tragedy of his father's death.

The day after he lost his father, Bauer flew home to Sacramento to be with his family. The coaches gave the team Monday off and Tuesday was the normal free day of an NFL regular-season week.

"They said just to take care of it and come back if you want for practice," Bauer said. "We would love to have you this week, but you do what you have to do."

What Bauer didn't do was spread the news to his teammates about losing Big Hank. After helping his family make the funeral arrangements, he flew back to San Diego that Tuesday night and practiced on Wednesday and Thursday.

"I fly back up there on Thursday night and I miss practice on Friday when we had the funeral," he said. "It was the first practice I had ever missed and everyone is thinking, 'OK, did he get cut?' You know how it is when you're not there, and I was a nobody."

But he was somebody to his teammates. Word leaked why Bauer skipped Friday's workout—because he had lost his father.

"We have the service and after it we were just sitting around the house," Bauer said. "It was brutal and I'm getting choked up talking about it.

"Then we hear a knock on the door and there was a guy there with a delivery. The players had passed around a hat for our family. We were not very well off, and that is putting it mildly. We were struggling.

"But inside the card was a check for $5,000. It was so unbelievable because I was a nobody. I was an undrafted rookie who just kept his head down, didn't say anything, and just tried to always do my job."

That job seemed to be beckoning for Bauer's return.

"I called my coach [Tommy Prothro] on Saturday and said I wanted to play tomorrow against the Cleveland Browns," Bauer said. "He said if I could get there by curfew on Saturday night, I could play in the game."

Bauer made curfew, then made personal history. He caught his first touchdown pass, from future Hall of Famer Dan Fouts, no less.

"It was a little shuffle pass of 15 yards," Bauer said.

It was a no-brainer that Bauer would get the game ball from the 37–14 victory. But Bauer asked equipment manager Sid "Doc" Brooks to put something special on it, other than Bauer's milestone catch and the final score.

"I wanted him to put every one of my teammates' names on it because of what they did for me," Bauer said of the ball, which also noted was in honor of Big Hank. "And I get choked up every time I think about it."

So do others when learning what happened to the game ball.

"I gave it to my mom," Bauer said. "On Mother's Day."

Chapter 9

ROLF BENIRSCHKE

Chargers at Dolphins—January 2, 1982

BIRTH DATE:	February 7, 1955
HOMETOWN:	Boston, Massachusetts
RESIDENCE:	Del Mar, California
JERSEY NO.:	6
POSITION:	Placekicker
HEIGHT:	6-foot-0
WEIGHT:	171 pounds

The Run-Up

Rolf Benirschke's teammates were ecstatic to see him. Oddly their faces showed shock instead of happiness.

"I had lost 65 pounds and was down to 122 pounds," Benirschke said. "I had wire sutures, an inch and half thick, holding me together. I looked like Frankenstein."

But he never looked back when entering the Chargers locker room in 1979 after his life-saving surgery on his diseased colon.

"I could hardly walk," Benirschke said. "So they arranged for me to have a seat in one of the executive boxes."

But Rick Smith, then the Chargers' director of public relations, heard the players' chatter once they learned Benirschke was at the stadium. Could the popular Benirschke come down to the locker room for a visit?

Benirschke, who days before was released from the hospital, was reluctant to honor their request.

"I didn't know if I could make it," he recalled. "I made it to the elevator and then I shuffled down to the locker room. I walk in there and you could see the look on [the] faces of these guys. It was like, 'Oh my gosh.' Their eyes got really big because I was a skeleton of a man they had not seen in two months."

Benirschke looked sickly and was wearing an ostomy (an external pouch) to collect his body fluids.

Though the extent of the issue was unbeknownst to his welcoming teammates. "They knew I was sick, but they really didn't have any idea," he said. "I said 'Hello' to everyone, but very gently."

Boisterous defensive tackle Louie Kelcher had another idea and leaped from his chair, heading for coach Don Coryell's office.

"We should make Rolf captain for this game and let him go out for the coin toss," Kelcher told Coryell.

Equipment manager Sid "Doc" Brooks sprung into action. He found an old No. 6 Benirschke jersey and slipped it over the ailing kicker's head.

Considering how much weight Benirschke had shed, it hung on him as if he was a small coat hanger.

That's when Benirschke came clean with Kelcher.

"I don't know if I can make it to midfield," Benirschke said.

"Well if you can't make it, I will carry you," the 6-foot-5, 291-pound Kelcher replied.

Benirschke, still in considerable pain, gingerly reached the sidelines on his own, careful not to be jostled.

"No one had really seen me and I start walking out on the field," Benirschke said. "Obviously I was walking very slowly."

Chargers fans noticed the man inside the jersey. With each small step Benirschke took, another spectator realized the man who had been fighting for his life was headed for the coin toss.

Waiting for him with the referees were the Pittsburgh Steelers' Jack Lambert and "Mean" Joe Greene. The roar grew.

"Man, these fans must really love you," Greene told Benirschke.

"I'll never forget the cheers in that stadium," Benirschke said. "It seemed like everyone was standing and cheering.

"They were pulling for a guy that was hurting. I don't know if those fans will ever know the impact that really had on my life. There were tears in my eyes as I was just overwhelmed by the kindness of people."

Benirschke was also floored by reality.

"I figured that was the last time ever I would be on a football field," he said. "I never thought I would play again."

But during the following months Benirschke got stronger. He regained his strength, weight (up to 187 pounds), and confidence. Before the 1980 Chargers training camp, he approached owner Gene Klein about trying out for his old job.

"I was healthy for the first time in a year and a half," Benirschke said. "He said if I can convince the medical staff that I can protect myself, then go ask Coryell."

Benirschke was wearing two external pouches at the time. But Coryell gave him his blessing and told him just to avoid contact during the summer session.

Fast-forward to that summer's Hall of Fame Game in Canton, Ohio. On a 95-degree day with an equally high humidity reading, Benirschke was anxious to show he was fit.

But at halftime he had to race to the locker room to fix an external pouch, which was malfunctioning in the oppressive heat.

"I'm thinking, *oh this is great*," he said.

But the game was tied in the fourth quarter and Benirschke was eager to supply the game-winner.

"This is [the] beginning of my comeback," he said. "But just as I lined up for the field goal, the heavens open up and the rain starts. The thunder is so loud because it is so close and the referees call the game."

But in the third preseason game, fate smiled on Benirschke. Just before halftime, the Chargers were near midfield and Benirschke would need to kick a 55-yarder.

"I'm thinking I can make this field goal," he said. "So the field-goal team goes running out."

Then a coach shouted "Punt team!"

Benirschke didn't hear him, or that's the story he tells.

"We were already out there so it was too late," he said, with a laugh. "And we make the kick, 55 yards, for the longest of my career. It was a sign to the coaches that they could treat me like a regular kicker and not some injured guy."

Benirschke had earned his roster spot.

"The Lord gave me the opportunity to make that kick and to play for an owner and a coach who were willing to take a chance," he said.

"I had a second chance to play football. But I also realized that it was a miracle they let someone do that with an ostomy bag on his side."

The Game

By Rolf Benirschke

I picked our playoff win over the Miami Dolphins in overtime during the 1981 season for a lot of reasons. It was just a classic game, the ebb and flow of it, but it was also a parallel of my life.

I should have died really when I was sick. I was very lucky to live. I got a second chance to live and a second chance to play football.

So to miss a kick in overtime and to get a second chance, the game was a parallel to my life.

The 27-yard kick I missed in overtime was close, but what some don't remember is they called for the field goal on second or third down. We were deep into overtime and guys were exhausted. When they called for the field goal, a lot of guys didn't get the word. So we were short three guys and we had to yell for them to come out.

I go to Ed Luther, my holder, and said, "We've got to call time out because we're short." But I thought, *well, we'll just kick it,* and I missed it.

Part of what made me so angry about it was knowing that I didn't control the situation better. If I would have turned around to call time out, the snap might have come. All this stuff was going on so fast and I just missed it after trying to get everyone lined up to kick it. I pulled it wide left. The snap was good and Ed's hold was good, but I just rushed it.

I was obviously disappointed. But I was angrier because I felt like I had let the team down. It was an awful, awful feeling because I didn't have the courage to call time out. I should have called time out. I don't want that to ever be an excuse because there is no excuse. It was unforgivable, really.

I was so angry when I got to the sidelines because I knew I would never get another chance. [Chargers linebacker] Jim Laslavic was the only guy that was willing to talk to me and he said, "You are going to get another chance." I said "Right, when hell freezes over I'll get another chance."

Then five or six minutes later we march down the field and had a chance to kick again. I just remember I was so grateful. Oh my gosh, I was walking out there again and I was just so excited to do it.

It was weird when we made the 29-yard kick to win the game. The Orange Bowl went absolutely quiet. It was almost like you couldn't hear anything.

I go to Ed, "It was good, right?" I turned to the bench and those guys are jumping off the ground. It was just so eerie because it had been so loud in Miami with it being such an epic game. You can actually see me in the video turning to Ed and saying, "Did it go in?"

I really hit it well. I killed it. It was such a good feeling.

To get a second chance was so satisfying.

When we marched down for it we called for the field goal unit on second down. And this time, we were ready, of course.

But when you look at the replay, our right wing back misses a block. I'm not going to say who it is because he is a good friend. No one will know except him and those that look at the video.

But the [Miami defender] splits the end and wing back and he could have blocked the kick. If you look at the video, he is pounding the ground afterward. He could have got there.

It was such a great feeling of redemption because the team had fought so hard.

The Aftermath

Rolf Benirschke likely kicked the most famous field goal in Chargers history. His 29-yard, overtime boot to beat the Miami Dolphins in the 1981 playoffs is etched in Chargers lore.

He put the Chargers four quarters shy of their first Super Bowl, even if they stumbled the following week in the Freezer Bowl against the Cincinnati Bengals.

Benirschke didn't have a field goal in that game. But for every one he made in 1980 and through the rest of his San Diego stint, he brought his right leg back for a cause—Kicks for Critters—that was near and dear to his family's heart.

His father, Kurt, a one-time professor of pathology at Dartmouth, was the research director at the San Diego Zoo when Rolf started kicking for the Chargers.

"He's interested in endangered species, and so am I," Rolf Benirschke said. "So we started a Kicks for Critters campaign for research on endangered species. For every field goal I kick, I donate $50 to it and other people donate what they want."

Benirschke's reliable right leg raised thousands for animals that needed assistance. Of course, an NFL locker room being what it is, if Benirschke had a rough day he heard about that, too.

During one post-game cooldown, teammate Louie Kelcher, among Benirschke's best friends, didn't beat around the bush.

"I remember one game where I missed a couple field goals," Benirschke said. "And Louie says in a loud voice, 'Hey Rolf, how many animals died today because of those field goals you missed?'"

Kelcher was joking, we think.

But Benirschke was always serious about others—those with two legs as well as those getting around on four.

Benirschke said he learned that by being an athlete, he was afforded a platform few others could claim.

"It came from my agent, Leigh Steinberg, when I was coming out of college," Benirschke said. "He was a very bright guy and great counsel for me. He told me I had a great opportunity and he challenged all of his clients to take advantage of their higher calling, no matter where they played. That they had a chance to do something of real significance."

Thanks to the goodwill Benirschke formed with Chargers fans, San Diego's annual blood drive is another part of his legacy.

When Benirschke underwent life-saving surgery in 1979, San Diego's blood bank calculated that he used 78 pints of blood. So Benirschke started a blood drive later that year and was floored by the response.

For eight hours, hundreds stood in line at then-San Diego Stadium, in tribute to Benirschke and those in need.

"I turned on the TV news late that afternoon and it had film showing hundreds of people lined up at the stadium," he said.

"I told my mother, 'I didn't know they loved the Chargers that much,' and she said, 'It's not only the Chargers they love, those people love you, too.' I decided I had to go down there and thank those people myself, and I did. Now there's an annual Chargers blood drive."

Thousands of pints are collected each year, with countless lives affected because of Benirschke.

The 37th annual blood drive in 2015, the largest single-day event of its kind in the United States, collected 72,000 pints.

"And each pint can be used for one to four people," he said. "When I think about that, it is just so humbling."

Chapter 10

ED WHITE

Chargers at Bengals—January 10, 1982

BIRTH DATE:	April 4, 1947
HOMETOWN:	La Mesa, California
RESIDENCE:	Alpine, California
JERSEY NO.:	67
POSITION:	Guard
HEIGHT:	6-foot-1
WEIGHT:	269 pounds

The Run-Up

Ed White became one of the most celebrated guards in Chargers history. He was inducted into the team's Hall of Fame and named to its 40th and 50th anniversary teams.

Although his past also showed him lining up on the opposite side of the ball.

White was an All-American nose guard at the University of California. He was the focal point in the team's noted "Bear Minimum" defense.

But once he left college for a career in pro football, fate pointed him to Minnesota, where its defense required little assistance.

That made White a lineman of a different color.

"When I went to the Vikings, they had the 'Purple People Eaters,'" he said. "They specifically drafted me to play on the offensive line and I knew that. So that was the way it was and I learned how to play offensive guard.

"But secretly, I really wanted to play defense my whole career."

Although White, who would be inducted into the College Football Hall of Fame, couldn't keep his lips sealed. He constantly badgered Chargers coach Don Coryell to let him be the hammer instead of the nail. White longed to be the one delivering the big blows on ball-carriers, and finally, Coryell relented.

"Ironically, I got to play only two plays on the defensive line for the Chargers," White said. "It was in a game where the other team was down on the goal line."

In a big series White was asked to make a big play, and he did just that.

"The first play was really special," he said. "I made a tackle and it was for a loss."

See there, NFL? White could be a defensive bear somewhere other than in college. He was trying to show them that he had the agility, know-how, and attitude to halt runners in their tracks, and then some.

"That's what I'm thinking," White said.

Think again.

"On the next play I get too high with my body and they double-team me," White said, his boastful voice dropping an octave or two. "They ended up pinning me up against the goal post."

And on the next play?

It never came.

"That was the last time I played defense," he said, with a laugh.

And that was the last time Coryell heard a peep from his offensive lineman lusting for the defensive line.

Regrets, White had a few. But his 17-year NFL stint that featured him flipping to guard wasn't among them. Before landing with the Chargers, White was among only 11 Vikings to play in all four of their Super Bowls: IV, VIII, IX and XI.

"Looking back on it, I wouldn't have changed a thing," he said. "It was a good career. And if I would have played on defense, I probably wouldn't have played as long."

Then again, here came that twinkle in White's eyes.

"Defense," he said, "was always my first love."

The Game

By Ed White

After the Miami playoff overtime win we arrived back in San Diego in the middle of the night totally exhausted and drained, emotionally and physically.

Then we started preparing for the Bengals. We were warm-weather guys overly concerned about the cold. Sid "Doc" Brooks, our equipment man, was fitting guys for rubber scuba gloves and everything else, but we were trying to concentrate on the game. This was the big advantage that the Vikings always had, playing fair-weather teams in the playoffs.

We go into Cincinnati with sub-freezing conditions and we were ice skating on the field. The game resembled hockey more than football. The killer was [Bengals owner] Paul Brown opening the tunnel doors to create a huge draft when Dan [Fouts] and our offense were heading into the wind. The windchill was recorded at 80 below zero!

We had the best equipment man ever in Doc and he was doing everything to help us leading up to the game with equipment. But we had so much stuff on that I couldn't move. It was that cold and really that game should have been moved. But they don't take into consideration the health of the players,

We were kind of psyched out about it and we just didn't respond well to the whole thing, the way everybody was bundled up. The whole city was frozen. It was the coldest game I had ever played in. It was amazing.

The really tough part of that was they opened the tunnels to let the draft through when we had the ball. They opened the ends of the stadium when we were headed in a certain direction, with the wind in our face. Then they would close it when their guys had the ball. That was Paul Brown.

It was not football. We had rubber basketball shoes on and what we ended up playing, it just wasn't football. It wasn't a football game.

The ball was hard to hold on to. It was all we could do to run the ball and nobody wanted to hit the ground. It was as hard as a brick.

It took the game away from football, really. I understand playing conditions and playing outdoors; that's where the game belongs. But these were arctic conditions.

I wasn't really focused as much on the game as just trying to get through it. I think that was part of the problem. It didn't seem like football to me. It was not.

Talent-wise, we were the better team. Everyone knew about our offense. But that was the defense, too, where we had guys on the line like Fred Dean, Louie Kelcher, [and] Gary "Big Hands" Johnson. We had the secondary. We had the linebacking crew.

It was meant to be our year, up to that point.

The Bengals were a playoff team. They had skill and talent, like we had. But you couldn't run and our receivers couldn't do their thing. I don't remember a lot that was special about the game other than it was colder than crap. You were just trying to get through the game. It was that kind of a day.

I think the big thing was leading up to it; the game the previous week in Miami [41–38 in overtime] had sucked so much out of us. The emotion and the game itself, it was just so phenomenal. That was a pretty wild game and it just sucked a lot out of us players. We just weren't the same team in Cincinnati.

After that Miami game the reporters were interviewing us and I had a locker next to Louie Kelcher. A reporter asked Louie, "How do you feel?" He was from Texas and he said he felt like he rode a horse from coast to coast—we were just exhausted. The reporter said, "Ed, how do you feel?" I said, "I feel like I was the horse that Louie rode on."

Temperature-wise in Cincinnati, that was as incredible a game as there ever was. And the Miami game the week before in the heat and the humidity was on the other side of the thermometer compared to Cincinnati.

Then, of course, after we lost to the Bengals, 27–7, they got hammered in the Super Bowl. Our talent was so much better.

It was a bad situation and a bad idea to play. It was unfair. We were like ice cubes.

When you lose there is such an empty feeling that it really took us a while to get over it. You invest so much in a goal, in a season, and then, bam, it's over. So it was pretty dramatic.

We knew how good our team was and we knew we were a better team than Cincinnati, there is no question about that. And that is what makes it so tough.

The Aftermath

That loss to the Bengals never really left White. It stayed with him like frostbite, and just maybe there was a reason for that.

But playing in the game, and for the Chargers, lit a fire in White. It continued to burn after he retired in 1985, sparking an interest in coaching.

Ed White became Coach White at age thirty-nine.

"Coach [Don] Coryell approached me about it and I ended up being an offensive line assistant to coach Dave Levy," White said.

Levy's style and depth of knowledge resonated with White. White's days of putting his hand in the dirt were over, but Levy's down-to-earth approach won over White.

"I loved Coach Levy and the things that he taught me," White said. "It was natural for me to coach and I really liked it."

In an odd way, White's transformation years earlier from the defensive line to the offensive line paid dividends when a whistle found his lips.

"I had to be a technician because I had to really learn the techniques to survive," White said.

Like a sponge, the savvy White, a four-time Pro Bowler, absorbed the lessons he was taught. So when it came time to share his smarts, White was more than able.

"I had probably three of the finest NFL line coaches around in Bobb McKittrick, Jim Hanifan, and Dave Levy," White said. "They were all fabulous coaches and I was really blessed to be able to play for those guys in that time period. They were all different, but all really good. They taught it to me in a different way."

Like any coach, White started bouncing around at different locales.

"I went back to college at Cal and worked for Tom Holmoe," he said.

"Then I coached with Ted Tollner at San Diego State and he got fired. Ted told me then that coaches are just working until they get fired. Because at some point you're not going to be able to meet the expectations. There are very few long-termed coaches anymore."

White left coaching in 1998 when stepping away from SDSU.

"I would probably still be coaching if you didn't have to watch so much film," he said. "After that, I was pretty much done with coaching."

But he continues to reap its rewards.

"I still communicate with the players all the time," White said. "That's the best part about it."

Chapter 11

JIM LASLAVIC

Chargers at Dolphins—November 20, 1980

BIRTH DATE:	October 24, 1951
HOMETOWN:	Pittsburgh, Pennsylvania
RESIDENCE:	Coronado, California
JERSEY NO.:	54
POSITION:	Linebacker
HEIGHT:	6-foot-2
WEIGHT:	237 pounds

The Run-Up

Jim Laslavic was hard-headed as a stout linebacker. But it was a weak ankle that likely led to the game of his life.

Laslavic was a staple on the Detroit Lions' defense from 1973–77. A former third-round pick from Penn State—Linebacker U—Laslavic was the Motor City's reliable run-stuffer in the middle.

He wasn't flashy or spectacular, instead just good ol' steady. He was the type of player that was easy to coach and hard to get rid of.

Even so, Laslavic's sixth year had him in San Diego, but only because of a twist of fate—and a twist of an ankle.

"In the final game of my fourth season I turned my ankle against the Rams," Laslavic said. "It was in the third quarter and the trainer took a look at it."

He didn't like what he saw.

"You're done for the day," he told Laslavic.

The stubborn Laslavic revolted.

"Done? Tape it back up and I'll get back in there," Laslavic told him. "What a mistake that was."

Laslavic returned, but soon his ankle wasn't his concern. On a blitz, Laslavic was the recipient of a chop block, which demolished his left knee.

"I just knew right away because my knee exploded," Laslavic said. "It was an illegal block and the tackle got me. I don't think he felt real bad about it."

After surgery Laslavic tried to return six months later. He was down a step and soon out as a starter.

"I lost the job to one of my best friends, Ed O'Neil, a teammate of mine at Penn State," Laslavic said. "Ed was a good linebacker and with me being a half-step slower, I knew there was no way I was going to get my job back."

With an itch to play, Laslavic requested to be moved during the offseason. He landed in San Diego, spent four seasons with the Chargers, and after retiring, became a local TV sports anchor for more than three decades.

Of course he had his game of his life along the way, in part because he refused to heed a trainer's words of caution.

"I always wondered about that," Laslavic said. "If I had taken the trainer's advice and stayed out of the rest of that game, my knee wouldn't have exploded. And if that wouldn't have happened, would they had ever traded me to San Diego?"

The Game

By Jim Laslavic

That was the season I was backing up all three linebackers after missing the previous season in 1979 with another knee injury. So my ticket to making the team was to impress on them that I could play all three linebacker spots and special teams.

I think we only carried five linebackers that year because that team was, as you might remember, very heavily oriented to the offense. If I could do all that, they could save another roster spot for another offensive player. But I had been a middle linebacker in Detroit for five years.

This game was on a Thursday night, which was kind of odd back then. And it was back and forth.

We were tied at the half, and then we took the lead in the second half, and then they came back and tied it. Then it was Rolf [Benirschke] to the rescue, which was often the case.

JIM LASLAVIC

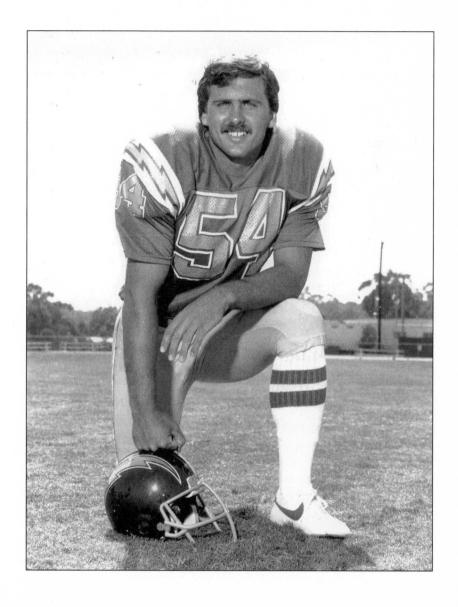

We won 27–24, in overtime, when he kicked a 28-yard field goal.

Dan Fouts didn't throw for over 300 yards and David Woodley went for 251. That was a terrific game and our team was such a great team, the best one I ever played on.

Then in the game, Ray Preston gets nicked up on the second or third play. So there I was as the backup, playing on the strong side, the left side, of our 4–3 defense.

When I ran out there I think [Miami] coach Don Shula's eyes must have lit up. He saw an inside linebacker playing on the outside.

So they kept running a particular trap play a lot to Tony Nathan. It involved me taking on the guard with the correct shoulder. But I had been coached up really well on how to defend it. But they were trying to pepper me with it.

The Dolphins thought they wanted to test me on that and of course, on the play-action, too. But it wasn't working and the tackles kept adding up. So I figured I was doing my job—I just figured it out.

Although on one play-action Nathan was wide open, five yards behind me. But Woodley overthrew him. Nathan looks at me with a smirk on his face saying, "You are one of the luckiest dudes I've ever met."

As the game went on I made a lot of tackles; they kept adding up. And that meant a lot to me. It was because I didn't want to be the weak link, even when they kept attacking me.

Also I just felt fortunate playing for the Chargers after I had sat out a year. Then to get some action with Ray out of that game, and then for a couple weeks after that, it was just great.

But that was the game in which I felt like everything had come full circle for me. I mean that was a make-or-break year for me, whether I was even going to make the team.

And in that game I had come back to play and to contribute to the team. I just wanted to play and enjoy it.

I knew I would never get that thrill again of competing like I had when I was back out there. To me, to be part of a winning team and to be in a supporting role, or any role at all, was extremely exciting.

The Aftermath

Jim Laslavic's game of his life was the snapshot of his career. He overcame odds to get on the field and when there, produced in a manner that endeared him to teammates and fans.

Not that the chant "Las-La-Vic" was ever on the lips of Chargers fans. Good thing, because they probably would have mispronounced it.

When Laslavic played for the Chargers' Tommy Prothro, Prothro butchered the name with regularity.

"One time I told him the proper pronunciation is 'Laz-la-vic,'" Laslavic said. "He took a deep drag from his cigarette and said, 'I'll give that some consideration.'"

San Diego's Don Coryell was famous for getting everyone's name wrong. That was true for Laslavic, who somehow became "Lasatick" or something along those lines.

"It wasn't even close," Laslavic said, with a hearty laugh.

What was near was the end of Laslavic's career. By any name, Coryell called him into his office after the 1981 season.

SAN DIEGO CHARGERS not, whatever

"Coach Coryell was leaning on his desk and he asked me to take a seat," Laslavic said. "He said, 'Thanks for all the hard work and we've appreciated it over the years, but we are going have to let you go.'

I had never been cut before so it was interesting," Laslavic said. "But a week later I had a job."

The Packers called. They had a spot for Laslavic and their proposal came with a hefty raise.

Laslavic played a year with Green Bay, but it was in a supporting role and his knee remained balky. After the 1982 season, Laslavic began working as a sports reporter for a San Diego TV station.

When the offseason gained on summer, Laslavic and his gimpy knee signed up for one more season.

But after agreeing to return in 1983, Laslavic was soon singing a different tune.

One Friday, San Diego's CBS TV affiliate reached out, inquiring if Laslavic would become its weekend sports anchor.

"It was a Friday," Laslavic recalled, "and they told me they needed my answer by Monday."

Laslavic called John Meyer, his defensive coordinator in Green Bay, and informed him of his dilemma. Meyer told him he would hold Laslavic's roster spot, but he had to have a definitive answer pronto.

Sunday morning arrived and Laslavic did what he normally did: went to Sunday Mass near his Coronado residence, just across the bay from San Diego.

But this service would be unlike others, with Laslavic perplexed on which direction to point his life: back to the NFL with Green Bay or toward the sports media world.

Laslavic took his seat in a pew, his eyes trained straight ahead. But something told him to turn around, and he was amazed by the sight.

"Two rows behind me is Joe Paterno, his wife, Sue, and a couple of their kids," said Laslavic, surprised to see his college coach.

"We walked out of church and he didn't even say, 'Hello Jimmy.' Instead it was, 'When are you going to retire? I worry about you guys after you have played a long time like you. You have played long enough.'"

Destiny had found Lasalvic again.

Much like him hurting his knee in Detroit would lead him to being traded to San Diego for the game of his life, here was his former Penn State coach in the unlikeliest of places.

"After he said that I looked up to the heavens," Laslavic said. "And I looked back at Joe and said, 'I'm going to retire tomorrow.'

"He said, 'Great, how is the family?'"

Laslavic still shakes his head regarding that transformational morning.

"He was in town to give a speech and had not announced his arrival in Coronado to me," Laslavic said. "So when I saw him my eyes lit up. Then when he said what he said, well it was either a wonderful coincidence or it was fate."

Chapter 12

BILLY RAY SMITH JR.

Dolphins at Chargers—September 7, 1986

BIRTH DATE:	August 10, 1961
HOMETOWN:	Fayetteville, Arkansas
RESIDENCE:	Del Mar, California
JERSEY NO.:	54
POSITION:	Linebacker
HEIGHT:	6-foot-3
WEIGHT:	231 pounds

The Run-Up

Billy Ray Smith Jr.'s trek to the NFL started as a youngster, after his dad cleared a path in his home.

"We would move all the furniture out of the dining room," he said. "Dad and [I] would practice. He was teaching me about hand speed, how to get past the guard, how to take on the center. Right there in my dining room."

Smith had a knowledgeable dad showing him the ropes: Billy Ray Smith Sr.

The elder Smith, an NFL standout, introduced his son to football. Smith Jr. was born in 1961, the year his father was traded by the Pittsburgh Steelers to the Baltimore Colts.

That was on the eve of the Colts' heyday, with stars such as quarterback Johnny Unitas and running back Lenny Moore. Smith Sr., a defensive end and tackle, joined a nasty front which included Art Donovan, Gino Marchetti, and later, Bubba Smith.

"I was born into all of that," Smith Jr. said.

His dad's NFL life was due as much to his tenacity as his strength. At 6-foot-4, 230 pounds, Smith Sr. was considered undersized. But the one-time Golden Gloves regional champion compensated for it with a toughness that wasn't lost on his impressionable son.

He noticed it during those football lessons in the living room, while Smith Jr.'s mother turned the other way.

"She didn't really care," the younger Smith said. "At least I was out of her hair."

That was especially true during training camps. It was a daily ritual that Smith, starting at six years old, was deposited at Western Maryland University, where the Colts practiced.

"It was unbelievable," he said. "I would spend every day that I could there and that was almost every day. It was like my day care."

Most didn't care that the little Smith was around. Then again, steely coach Don Shula wasn't among those shrugging his shoulders.

"Shula would yell at me if I ever walked on the field," Smith Jr. said. "He would say, 'Little Rabbit, get off the field!'"

Little Rabbit?

"They called my dad 'Br'er Rabbit' which came from his initials B. R. and they just shortened it to Rabbit," Smith Jr. said. "That made me 'Little Rabbit' and I loved it. Man, that was a ton of fun."

Much of that joy came from Smith Sr. He was a gregarious man, quick with a back slap and a joke. He almost always played the game with intensity but with a joy as well, a fact that made Super Bowl III stand out to this day for Smith Jr.

Joe Namath's Jets upset his daddy's Colts and the kid was astonished by Smith Sr.'s postgame reaction.

"He was sitting at his locker and he still had his T-shirt on under his pads and he was wearing his shorts," Smith Jr. said. "And he was just sitting there biting his thumb. I had never seen him so quiet. Usually he was boisterous, hilarious—typical Southern, saying 'How you doing?'

"But he was so quiet and that lasted for a week or two. You better believe it I made sure my bed was made and we had the best-mowed lawn on the block during that time.

"Super Bowl III haunted him to the grave. I had never, ever seen him like that and he never got over it."

The final game for Smith Sr. came in Super Bowl V, when the Colts beat the Cowboys. After that, the elder Smith became a stockbroker but he watched his son as closely as he watched the market.

Like his dad, Smith Jr. went on to become an All-American at Arkansas.

And when Smith Jr. was drafted by the Chargers in 1983, the elder Smith often came to San Diego.

"He had some clients out here and he would bring them to the games," he said. "I always imagined him saying, 'Yep, that's my boy right there.'"

After any competition, the two Smiths put their heads together.

"It was the same as my first year in Pop Warner [youth football]," Smith Jr. said. "He would take me aside and say, 'This is what you did really good. And this is what you did really bad, just in case they did it the next time. So try this and do that.'

"It was like that all the way through my career. Whether he saw the game on TV or live, he could break it down and tell me the things I was supposed to be doing. He always knew exactly what the other team was trying to do offensively; he had a great eye."

An overbearing football father? Not to Smith Jr.

"I loved it," he said. "To have that kind of a football mind watching over you and being able to share thoughts on what happened, and if it happened again or if they bring that same kind of blocking scheme. I knew how to take care of it."

Smith Sr. prepared his son for everything—save the first time a 6-foot-7, 280-pound rookie named Bubba Smith entered the Colts' facility in 1967.

"Bubba Smith walked up next to dad's locker and I started crying," Smith Jr. said. "I was used to NFL-sized players but he was so much bigger than everyone else that I just started tearing up. My dad had to take me over to the trainer's room and tell them to take care of me for a little while."

The Game

By Billy Ray Smith Jr.

It was that Miami game [in 1986] because after three years of just getting beat up as an inside linebacker, they moved me back outside. It was a chance to rush the passer again, make some big plays and then to be able to do it against Dan Marino was special. We just killed them in that game, 50–28, it was hilarious.

Dan and I had come out the same year in 1983 and we had done all the Kodak All-American trips and all the other things together. We were buddies.

So it was a lot of fun with the new defense that was put in. It let me get up the field a little bit and jump a few quarterbacks. It was good stuff.

We stayed in an odd front, but it was more of a multiple-front defense. So I would play on the open side or opposite the tight end side.

I had been standing in front of 330-pound nose tackles, playing against guys that weren't my size.

So when they made the change at defensive coordinator before the season, bringing in Ron Lynn for Dave Adolph, it was really nice.

They brought in a new staff on the defensive side and that changed the way we were playing defense. That was just about the time Air Coryell was ending.

I loved going back on the outside as a linebacker but I never complained about being inside. I was raised by an NFL defensive tackle [Billy Ray Smith Sr.] and he told me, "Wherever they put you, just be thankful you have a job."

But that game against Dan was neat. It was the first game of the season, we were at home and I got two sacks.

I remember I got one early and that I just wanted a piece of him so bad. I was just after him all day after they finally put in that kind of defense that would get after the passing attack.

If they didn't have a two tight-end formation I would get to go to the side that just had the offensive tackle.

Lee Williams had a sack; so did Leslie O'Neal. We had a pretty good defense.

We had played each other one other time over the previous three years and we would run into each other over the years. But that year it was the opener and we were going against a Miami offense that was certainly one of the most well-respected in the league. And Dan was the reason it was so respected.

He was so hard to sack because of the way he let go of the ball. He never had to wind up to throw the ball. He had such a strong arm that once he brought the ball to his ear, it was gone. The guy was just a great quarterback and a great leader.

And in knowing him so well, it was extra special to sack him. When you get up after you sack the quarterback, you push him a little more, especially with it being Marino. You hear the air leaving his lungs.

And the game was special because it was the opener and we have a new defensive coordinator and a new defense. We had different players lined up in different places.

In the preseason, we didn't give it away with what we were going to do. Those [coaches] did a great job putting that defense in.

And we had the personnel to make the scheme work at that point and time. In that game it was absolutely a necessity to get to the quarterback and rough him up a little bit. Getting after Dan, that was pretty much what we were shooting for the whole time. Although they had a good running back in Tony Nathan. But getting after Dan, that was just fine with me.

We had played Dan before, but I don't remember that game. What that means is if we beat the Dolphins, I remember it. If they beat us, I don't. I just remember the games where we played well and we won. Life is a lot easier that way.

I remember that Dan had slipped in the draft we were in. All I knew was that everybody was wishing the Chargers could have drafted him to be sitting behind Dan [Fouts] and just have him come in as soon as Dan retired, but that didn't happen.

Marino was a great guy with a great sense of a humor for a quarterback. He was really sharp and had a great wit, which of course made it so much fun to sack him!

Then when we started off and we won that first game, we thought, *We got this figured out.* That was the game Gary Anderson had that classic vault into the end zone for a touchdown.

Then we go two months without a win. That was a long drought.

The Aftermath

Billy Ray Smith was a junior to his dad, Billy Ray Smith Sr.

But mention Junior to Smith and he thinks of just one: Junior Seau.

Not since Smith was selected out of Arkansas in 1983 had the Chargers drafted a linebacker in the first round. But when the Tampa Bay Buccaneers took Keith McCants with the fourth pick in the 1990 NFL Draft, San Diego general manager Bobby Beathard couldn't shout "Junior Seau" fast enough.

"I had never seen anything like him, never," Smith said, his eyes growing wide when recalling Seau. "It was his athletic ability, absolutely.

"But he was also so unbridled. He wouldn't necessarily listen very much in how the defense was supposed to work. If he got out on the field and could see a way to make it work better, he would do that. Any time Junior had an idea it usually worked.

"Compared to anybody else, his athleticism was unbelievable and he was a fantastic teammate."

Seau and Smith were both linebackers, but their connection also went deeper. Much like a younger Smith had to adjust to a different scheme, so did this Tasmanian devil from USC, who was going a million miles an hour in a million different directions.

Smith, who would become a member of the team's 40th and 50th anniversary teams, was entering his eighth year in the league in 1990. He wasn't shy about taking Seau under his wing. That is, when he could get Seau to stand still, of course.

"I felt for him because he was going through what I went through," Smith said. "He was an outside linebacker and he became a weak side, inside linebacker. I was feeling for Junior.

"I never saw him struggle, but I know how difficult the change of position was. I talked to him about it."

Seau listened, nodded, and then went about knocking ball-carriers on their backsides.

"I'm telling you he took that position over and he made it his," Smith said. "I had never seen anyone play that position the way he played it."

It was Seau's mixture of skill and determination that Smith appreciated. Smith, after battling injuries for three seasons, wasn't nearly as mobile as Seau—few were. So if Seau was causing havoc, there was a piece of Smith riding along on Seau's pads.

"It was his instincts and he was such a gifted athlete," Smith said. "Junior didn't necessarily stick to the game plan. If he saw this or saw that, to his credit, if he saw a chance to make a play he would make it. And they were normally plays behind the line of scrimmage. It was really unfair to those guys on the offensive side of the ball."

Smith was a solid teacher. But considering the pupil, Smith had a good chance to shine as an instructor.

"I taught him as much as I could but he was playing a different game," Smith said. "He was so fast, so strong; just the combination of size and speed.

"It was watching a guy who looked like he was trying to drive the defensive coordinator crazy because every single play you never knew where Junior was going to go. And he would make all the plays because he could blow up three guys at one time. He was strong as hell."

Then Smith's voice catches in his throat. Any reminiscing of Seau comes with a remembrance of his death, which still shakes Smith.

Seau committed suicide in 2012, putting a gun to his chest that delivered a bullet that tore through the heart of every Chargers player and fan.

"I feel terrible for not having done anything about it," Smith said. "That I didn't see what he was going through and didn't sit down with him and talk about it a little bit. I just didn't know. But really none of us did."

When word of the shooting reached Smith, his knees buckled.

"I know I had to sit down because it hit me so hard," Smith said. "He was just a great guy."

And one that Smith stressed deserves a grand story to end the conversation.

To that effect, there's a tradition among the Chargers that the first-round pick gets stuck with a significant dinner tab during training camp.

A naive Smith had the check plopped in his lap in 1983.

"After practice one day Dan Fouts pulled up in his Mercedes," Smith said. "He said, 'Hey, you want to go to dinner with me and some of the guys?'"

Smith did a double-take.

"Man, Dan Fouts wants me to go to dinner?" Smith said. "I couldn't believe it."

At Bully's Restaurant the offensive starters were salivating over the menu when Fouts and Smith strolled in. After a grand dinner with numerous beverages, everyone walked out when Smith went to the restroom.

When Smith returned, he was suddenly sitting at a table for one.

"Not only did I have to pay the bill, but without a ride I was late getting back to camp and was fined," Smith said.

So when Seau arrived in 1990, Smith was that year's architect of making the rookie pay off the field as well as on it.

"We went to this steak place with all the linebackers and let's just say linebackers can eat a lot of food," Smith said.

The bill came and the savvy Seau just smiled as the evening's final course of crow was served to Smith.

"During the day in the locker room Junior had taken my American Express card out of my wallet without me knowing about it," Smith said. "So he had paid the bill with my credit card. It was hilarious.

"I thought, *This isn't your normal, everyday rookie linebacker.*"

Chapter 13

BURT GROSSMAN

Chiefs at Chargers—January 2, 1993

BIRTH DATE:	April 10, 1967
HOMETOWN:	Philadelphia, Pennsylvania
RESIDENCE:	San Diego, California
JERSEY NO.:	92
POSITION:	Defensive end
HEIGHT:	6-foot-4
WEIGHT:	270 pounds

The Run-Up

The Chargers' representative was there to collect Burt Grossman, and was that really Jim Mora?

"He was a gopher back then," Grossman said of Mora, a future NFL and college head coach. "He picked me up at the airport after I got drafted and that was it. There was no media, no nothing."

Grossman's best memory from first stepping foot in San Diego in 1989? It came when exiting Lindbergh Field.

"The biggest thing for me was the sign pointing toward 'Los Angeles' when we left the airport. "I thought, *Wow, Los Angeles.* It didn't say anything about San Diego," Grossman said with a laugh.

Grossman said plenty during his five-year San Diego stay. His mouth was open as often as Air Coryell receivers.

In 1990, Grossman graced the *Sports Illustrated* cover, with a story titled "Big Mouth." Never shy, Grossman was a favorite of sportswriters and fans with his outspoken approach and quirky attitude.

Dan Henning, the Chargers' coach at that time, wasn't impressed with Grossman's press clippings. During the 1990 offseason workouts, Henning speculated Grossman could be better suited for a backup role, which riled up Grossman.

"Dan Henning has never been to a defensive meeting," Grossman said. "He's never seen defensive film. He can't spell defense, and you're gonna believe him?

"He doesn't know who is playing. He sits in that offensive meeting room all day yelling in that New York accent. I sat with him for a TV thing before a game with Joe Namath and Dan couldn't name our starting 11 on defense."

Typically, Grossman pushed the right buttons to get a response.

"Anything Grossman has to say isn't going to bother me," Henning fired back. "He gets on me for the way I dress. Look at him; what does he think he is, some sort of oil painting?"

Grossman was far from a paint-by-numbers person. He was outlandish with everyone, including those writing his paychecks. In addition to taking shots at Henning, he pointed barbs at the front office.

"I don't want to say the Chargers don't want to win, but you look at some teams like San Francisco and they're paying backup quarterback [Steve Young] $2 million a year," Grossman said. "Well, you have to say that team obviously wants to win. They're dishing out $6 million a year just on quarterbacks [Young and Joe Montana]. That's our whole payroll just about.

"You got teams like Dallas, who want to win, spending more money every year. If there's somebody out there available, someone seems to always come up with the money, and it's always somebody like Al Davis. You don't think we needed Ronnie Lott?

"I mean if you want to be a great art collector you don't do all your shopping at the flea market. You get players like [Leslie] O'Neal and then you just put up with all his weird stuff."

Well before landing on *SI*'s cover, Grossman plopped himself into Mora's car. An organizational errand-runner had found the Chargers' latest big fish.

That Grossman came ashore in San Diego raised eyebrows, including his own.

Grossman met with and worked out for clubs before the draft after starring at Pittsburgh—but not the Chargers.

In the draft's build-up, not a word from San Diego reached Grossman, regarding interest the club might have.

"I didn't know the Chargers were going to pick me," he said. "I never got a call from the general manager or anything."

That silence continued after the Chargers selected Grossman number 8 overall in the epic 1989 NFL draft.

"You know how when you're watching it on TV and the team usually calls the guy a minute before it takes him?" Grossman asked. "I got nothing. A reporter called me before the Chargers did. That should have told me something right there."

It was a draft for the ages, with four of the first five draftees having Pro Football Hall of Fame careers: Troy Aikman, Barry Sanders, Derrick Thomas, and Deion Sanders.

"Detroit flew me in and we all knew they were going to take Troy Aikman or Barry Sanders," Grossman said. "But they still bring you in."

"Going into the draft we had a pretty good idea who the picks were going to be," Grossman said. "It was just a matter of where they would go."

Grossman went in the top 10 and still curses his fate and timing.

"I look back that if I would have stayed an extra year at Pitt and how much money I would have made going higher the next year," he said. "I would have gone from being in the greatest draft in history to one of the worst drafts in history."

Grossman, as usual, had a point and didn't mind sharing it.

The Game

By Burt Grossman

Mine was the Kansas City game when we beat them, 17–0, in San Diego in the 1992 playoffs.

I think it was my greatest game, but not for the obvious reasons.

I thought about it and the obvious reasons would have been the year we played the Eagles because I'm from Philadelphia.

But really that game didn't mean much, because, well the game didn't mean much.

So that playoff game was the first game where it was really significant here. We hadn't been to the playoffs in probably 100 years—ever since the Fouts era pretty much and this was in the '80s.

Just all that played into it; we had been so bad here. My first year we were 6–10, then 4–12 and we always had a high draft choice. But the games didn't really mean anything.

Although all the games up to that point, we started off 0–4, so I guess they all kind of meant something because you had to win out to get into the playoffs.

We were a wild card with 11 wins, think about that! That's how much better the division was back then—11 wins, you get the wild card and no bye.

So it was more because of that. I'm sure there was that kind of atmosphere here in San Diego with Fouts and those people. But it wasn't anything that anyone had experienced in 10 years.

It felt different for a few reasons.

Like it never rains here and it rained that day. It was the only game in San Diego I had ever been to or played in that it rained, which was funny in its own right.

It was weird back then in San Diego.

The 49ers were a dynasty pretty much still and we had the Raiders in L.A. who had like Bo Jackson, Tim Brown, and Ronnie Lott and they were still good. We even had the Rams then.

Up until that playoff game, it was like we were just this after-thought; we were Tijuana's team, pretty much.

And we really were because the big markets had the other three teams and we were just an afterthought.

I guess that game was the first big one for us; there was no *Monday Night Football* or Sunday night games for us. Unless they wanted to see someone beat up on us, like Rocky Balboa and Apollo Creed. But that was the first game that really meant something.

Sadly it took like until my fourth year to play in a game that meant something.

It's mostly because the others didn't mean anything because we were so bad. And we had been as bad as the franchise had ever been to that point. It was a sad point for the franchise. You just don't realize it at the time.

I remember when I first got here my rookie year, just on our defensive line, we had something like 60-some sacks. Some crazy number and we got used to [it].

Shawn Lee had 15 sacks my rookie year, I had 10 or 11, Leslie O'Neal like 12. We had those three guys and two or three others sprinkled in.

I think in that playoff game we had 10 sacks—something crazy.

I had 2 ½ and Leslie had two and an interception. Lee had two sacks.

We are always pretty good on defense but not on offense.

If we would have Philip Rivers then, good lord. We had Anthony Miller, Rod Bernstein, Ronnie Harmon, and we had all these people but no one to get them the ball. Stan Humphries was the first guy who could actually get the ball to somebody.

We had this long line of people that weren't very good and then along came Stan and he could actually complete a pass. We had all these receivers, which were amazing, but can you imagine if we had Rivers on that team with those people?

But I remember we shut Kansas City out, which is rare in the NFL, let alone in a playoff game.

What I remember about the game was if I reached 10 sacks [in the regular season] I got a $25,000 bonus. I had missed three or four games that year and had 8 ½ sacks. Then I got 2 ½ sacks in the game but it didn't count because it wasn't the regular season. I do remember that, not getting $25,000 for getting all those sacks.

The Chiefs were similar to us. They had Derrick Thomas, Neil Smith, and Dan Salamaua, all those guys; they were real good on defense. They had Todd McNair and one other guy in the secondary. They drafted a first-rounder in Harvey Williams.

It was a defensive show—Leslie got an interception—and against a common opponent. We knew them as well as we knew ourselves.

I do remember it was such a big deal that whole week leading up to the game. It was like when the Padres went to the World Series in 1998. They got this same buildup and then they got beat and it was such a big letdown. So it was kind of the same with the buildup.

In the last game of the regular season we played the Raiders up in L.A. and we beat them. We came back on the bus and there was like 10,000 people out there. It was the first time they met you at the airport and all the stuff.

Sometimes people complain about the San Diego fans but they never put a winning product out there to get that connection. You have to put something out there that is good. You got to give them something they can watch.

So it was the first time there was Chargers fever in twelve, fifteen years, maybe longer. It was totally the opposite of what we were. It was almost like you see it in other places, you would turn on TVs and see all these other places have the atmosphere, but it was almost like we were in Tijuana. We had nothing like that.

Nobody even wanted to come to our training camp back then. There was like three people—the same crazy three people. There was no security, no ropes, nothing. Nobody really cared.

It all kind of changed after that playoff game. I think if we would have lost that game, it would have been different. We ended up getting blown out by Miami in Miami in another rainstorm the following week, but I don't know if that even mattered at that point.

It was like if you would have lost that one to Kansas City it would have been like Cincinnati or Marty Schottenheimer back then: you can't win a playoff game, you are a fraud again.

So that is why it was so important. That was the first playoff win and that kind of changed everything—although I don't think the following year we went to the playoffs. But it started to mushroom from that '92 playoff game. We got like "Inside the NFL" from HBO coming out and things like that.

But the year after that [1993] they went to the Super Bowl.

So it was the only playoff win I had and it was honestly the only game that really meant something.

The Aftermath

Burt Grossman was a steady player and a super quote for the media.

But Grossman wasn't around when the Chargers reached their lone Super Bowl to cap the 1994 season.

After 1993, Grossman was peddled to his hometown Philadelphia Eagles.

Instead of being happy, Grossman longed for the Chargers—or at least the style of offenses he was accustomed to combating.

"Why isn't everyone passing the ball?" Grossman said about the NFC East's ground-and-pound approach. "This sure isn't the AFC West."

He returned to San Diego with his wife, years later. Although their initial connection had come years earlier, in the week following Grossman's game of his life, when he had 2 ½ sacks in the Chargers' 17–0 postseason win over the Chiefs.

His wife happened to have been present when he and the team was preparing for a 1992 Miami playoff game. While Grossman was working ways to reach the quarterback, his future wife was fine-tuning her cheerleading moves.

"We went down there for a week to practice leading up to the Miami game," Grossman said of the 1992 AFC divisional showdown. "We practiced at St. Thomas Aquinas High in Fort Lauderdale.

"What is crazy was my wife was a 10th-grade cheerleader at that high school and they used to practice their cheerleading when we were practicing on the field."

Grossman quickly did the math and made a clarification.

"I didn't meet her then," he said. "Don't get me wrong. I met her in Miami in 2001 and we didn't realize it at the time that we were both at St. Thomas Aquinas at the same time."

Grossman, who retired in 1996 because of a neck injury, became Mr. Mom once he stopped playing. His wife was the breadwinner as a high school assistant principal in the San Diego area.

"We had kids so I just stayed at home," Grossman said. "I had no social life. Her social circle became my social circle and that was pretty much education."

That struck a chord with Grossman, who always had a soft spot for children.

And that extended well beyond raising his two boys.

Grossman coached football at San Diego's Hoover High, a rough-and-tumble school in the inner city. There he found countless teenagers needing advice—some of it football-related, some not.

"Some of those kids are eating hot Cheetos for dinner," Grossman said.

He talked football, but also gave tips that extended beyond the sidelines. He taught a life-skills class that, Grossman said, tried to recreate the kitchen table in someone's home.

Although Grossman's upbringing was hardly a scene ripped from an *Ozzie and Harriet* episode.

His mother left the family, unannounced.

His father was more concerned if his teams covered bets than pulling the covers over his son at night.

"But some of these [Hoover] kids live in like a two-bedroom apartment with 11 people and some of them are sleeping on the kitchen floor," Grossman said. "Our place was like the *Little House on the Prairie* compared to what some these kids live in. And while our [family] money wasn't great, it wasn't terrible compared to what I see."

Grossman even made a political run, with kids on his mind. He fell shy in his bid for a seat on the Sweetwater Union High School District board.

Despite falling short, he continued to stand tall with teenagers other than his own.

He kept coaching at Hoover and sharing his love. The Grossmans opened their home and adopted Don Ndiaye, a talented Hoover athlete not all that familiar with football.

"He was homeless," Grossman said matter-of-factly.

But under Grossman's guidance, Ndiaye earned a University of Arizona football scholarship—after playing just six games his senior year.

Grossman later worked for the nonprofit Able/Disabled Youth Builders organization. It gave an advocate's voice to those needing someone to clear his throat and tell it like it is.

For the vocal and vivacious Grossman, that was way too easy.

"I love kids," he said.

Chapter 14

JOHN CARNEY

Oilers at Chargers—September 19, 1993

BIRTH DATE:	April 20, 1964
HOMETOWN:	Hartford, Connecticut
RESIDENCE:	Carlsbad, California
JERSEY NO.:	3
POSITION:	Placekicker
HEIGHT:	5-foot-11
WEIGHT:	185 pounds

The Run-Up

In his eleven years with the Chargers, Carney wore No. 3.

How appropriate.

"For three years [1987, '88, '89], well, I wouldn't say I was cut," Carney said with a mischievous grin. "Let's just say there were contracts that weren't fulfilled."

His Irish eyes are smiling and why not?

Carney got no more than three shots and a cot in training camps for the Cincinnati Bengals and Tampa Bay Buccaneers. There were failed tryouts with the Bengals, two with the Miami Dolphins, and one each with the Kansas City Chiefs, Atlanta Falcons, and Chargers.

He played five games with the Buccaneers in 1988–89, filling in briefly before falling out of favor.

In 1987, after leaving Notre Dame, Carney had been confident about his chances with the Bengals despite being undrafted.

"Every college player comes out thinking, *I'm ready for the NFL; this is going to be great. I'm going to step right in and take right off and be rookie of the year.*

"I'm sure I had that thought process along those lines, but I wasn't ready physically or mentally for the NFL game."

Carney was cut and for that, he's thankful.

"It was a blessing," he said.

Come again?

"If I had the opportunity early with Cincy, I may have fallen so hard that the league would say, 'He is just not NFL caliber; next on the list.'

"If you fall hard enough and you get that reputation, you pretty much get blackballed. So I was fortunate to have an opportunity and time to go back and work on my game. Physically, I needed to be stronger, more durable, and more consistent on field goals and kickoffs."

While Carney was being shown the door, time and again, he would do so only after taking notes. He was getting his master's in kicking and gleaning tips from the best.

"I learned an immense amount of information, and training techniques and preparation from all the veterans I got to compete with in all the tryouts and training camps I went to," he said.

"I had an opportunity to learn what the guys that were playing every Sunday were doing. I would learn from them and go back home to Florida and work on those aspects of my game.

"I was fortunate, in hindsight, that the road was long for me."

It finally weaved its way to San Diego in 1990, when he picked the Chargers over the Chiefs and attended training camp.

"Kurt Schottenheimer was the special teams coach in Kansas City and he had been at Notre Dame when I was there," Carney said. "And they were really upset with Nick Lowery after Marty's [Schottenheimer] first year in 1989. They didn't make the play-offs and Nick struggled.

"But he was a future [Chiefs] Hall of Famer and guys like that, if they have an off year, they are usually so solid the following year.

"Or I could come out here to San Diego and go against Fuad Reveiz. There just seemed to be a little bit more of an opportunity here, so I chose to come to San Diego."

But the Chargers went with Reveiz's experience instead of giving Carney a roster spot. They kept his number close by, though.

When Reveiz faltered at the start of the season, the Chargers told Carney that if by Week 5 he hadn't rebounded, Carney would become their kicker.

Then in Week 4, the Los Angeles Rams were desperate for a kicker after Mike Lansford strained his calf. Their coach, John Robinson, told Carney he remembered him from those Notre Dame-USC games when Robinson was coaching the Trojans.

But Carney knew he likely had another job lined up, soon, with the Chargers.

"The Rams said if the Chargers called me, they would release me and let me take that job," Carney said. "That was really cool of them."

But Carney felt the heat on game day, after requested by the Rams to wear the No. 18 he wore for the Fighting Irish.

"I wake up Sunday morning and it was in the paper that some temporary kicker is the first ever player to wear [former Rams quarterback] Roman Gabriel's number," Carney said. "Mike Lansford said, 'Wow, you got a lot of pull around here.'"

But when the Chargers pushed Reveiz aside the following week, Carney's three years of being kicked around finally came to an end.

The Game

By John Carney

We started the 1993 season and kicked six field goals against Seattle and we won, 18–12.

Then the second game was in Denver and John Kidd, my holder, got hurt. So John Friesz, who was our starting quarterback, became our holder.

John Friesz was not quite as experienced or had the skill level holding as John Kidd.

So we go into the Houston game, kick another six field goals, and we win the game, 18–17.

We were just kicking a ton of field goals.

In the process of playing the Houston game we tied and then broke the NFL consecutive field goal record, which was 28 set by Morten [Andersen], and then 29 was the new record.

And the record-breaking kick ended up being the game-winner against Houston, off the dirt.

Thanks to the San Diego Padres, I was kicking off the area around second base to win the game.

There is a picture of us kicking the field goal and the laces aren't where they are supposed to be—let's just put it that way.

We put the ball through the uprights, off the dirt, with the laces not being where they were supposed to be. But we got the job done and it was a lot of fun.

Because it was a game-winner we felt everything was going to speed up a little. Obviously the defense has more motivation to rush.

But John Friesz felt he didn't have time to mess with the football. He wanted to make sure he got it down to the right spot and the right lean. So in the picture of the kick you see no laces.

You want them at twelve o'clock but I know I didn't kick the laces, so they were probably at nine o'clock, which is probably the worst place to have them for a kicker because the ball wants to go left.

But because I was kicking off the dirt and going really low on the ball, it has a tendency to straighten out if you get really low on the ball—that's technical stuff.

We were fortunate and I trusted John and I trusted [long snapper] Sam Anno and our protection was fantastic.

I probably approached the game with the mentality of just to give John a fraction of a second more to get the ball down and give me a little better look at what we were kicking. Because it might not be as perfect as where John Kidd would have placed the ball down.

We kicked six field goals that game and the two longest ones were in the direction of the scoreboard, which usually is the more difficult direction to kick a long field goal at Qualcomm Stadium. Most of the long field goals at Qualcomm are kicked toward the locker room.

It's a kicker's dream to have a team that stalls in the red zone a lot. It drives the coaches crazy, but they can at least pull away with three points instead of a goose egg, so they get something for it.

It was a busy day. I was getting a lot of work. There wasn't a lot of dead time for me. I really enjoyed the opportunity and the challenge.

There had been some chatter, obviously, in the media about the consecutive streak record. So as a player I tried to do my best to put that on the shelf and not let that interfere with my preparation or the process of performing.

At times I really shied away from media or stats people throughout my career; people reminding me or informing me of streaks or records or patterns.

Of course the stadium announcer announces, "so-and-so has just tied the consecutive streak record."

It was late in the game for the fifth field goal, which was toward the scoreboard. The sixth field goal, the game-winner off the dirt toward the locker room, was in the last two minutes of the game.

I remember it was exciting for John Friesz. He was the starting quarterback and it was *Hey, we just won the game!* Obviously the starting quarterback had a lot to do with moving the ball up and down the field and putting us in position at the end.

I was actually more elated that we won the game. That was exciting because we started off the season pretty strong.

We thought we had a strong team and it's always exciting to get wins early in the season.

That was my first thought when I saw the ball go through the uprights. It was *Hey, another win for us. We're on a roll.*

Then [director of public relations] Bill Johnston grabbed me and said, "By the way, you got the record."

But it wasn't about the record; the game was on the line. Screw the record; we need to make the kick to win the game, so that can't be our focus.

There is kind of a hush in the stadium during a kick, regardless if you are away or home, because everyone takes a breath and waits for the result. Both sides of the field [seem to take a breath]; someone is going to win or someone is going to lose. Everyone kind of takes a breath.

Then if it's loud and it's a home game, that means you made it.

Then if it's not so loud and you're home, that's not so good.

The Aftermath

Carney had a rough start to life after becoming the record-holder.

"John Kidd came back the following week and I proceeded to miss the first field goal I kicked with him [holding]," Carney said with a laugh.

But it wasn't an indication of what lay ahead, as he became the Chargers' all-time scoring leader with 1,076 points. A two-time Pro Bowler, he would be named to the team's 40th and 50th anniversary teams.

Carney kicked for the Chargers through the 2000 season, seeing the organization reach its summit as well as its lowest low.

When the franchise advanced to its only Super Bowl following the 1994 season, Carney was there. When it lost its first 11 games in 2000, Carney was there.

If not for Carney's 52-yard field goal in the final minute against the Kansas City Chiefs on November 26 that year, the 1–15 Chargers might have been 0–16.

He would have three stints with the New Orleans Saints and also make stops with the Jacksonville Jaguars, Kansas City Chiefs, and New York Giants. With the Saints, he was still kicking at the age of forty-six. Like George Blanda, Carney played in an NFL-record four decades.

"I was very blessed, very fortunate," Carney said. "Like every career there are ups and downs and peaks and valleys, but you grow from both of those. You learn a lot about yourself."

In New Orleans, he saw firsthand the ravages of Hurricane Katrina. When New Orleans was still reeling, his game-winner against the Carolina Panthers in 2005 put smiles on the weary citizens' faces and landed Carney on the cover of *Sports Illustrated*.

It was also with the Saints that Carney started their Super Bowl-winning 2009 season as their kicker. He morphed into a kicking consultant position with New Orleans as it won the title. He briefly kicked for the Saints again in 2010 before calling it a career.

"It was fun and I loved every phase of my career and the challenge it presented," Carney said.

"Early on: Trying to prove to be consistent, dependable, and trustworthy.

"Middle of career: At my physical peak and thinking, *What can I do to perform at my best and maybe leave a mark in the books?*

"Then end of the career: How can I continue to perform at a high level on Sunday and adjust my training?"

Carney's firsthand knowledge led him to train others. At the Carney Kicking Camp in northern San Diego County he works with pro, college, and high school kickers and punters.

Carney preaches to his pupils for them to leave the field like he did when setting the NFL record for consecutive field goals.

"It was a very fun game but a little bit fatiguing on the emotional and physical levels," he said. "But this is what you hope for.

"I have it written on our walls at the facility, 'Exhausted and victorious.' To be able to leave the field or court or whatever, exhausted and victorious, that is what makes exhaustion worth it."

Chapter 15

NATRONE MEANS

Chargers at Raiders—October 11, 1998

BIRTH DATE:	April 26, 1972
HOMETOWN:	Harrisburg, North Carolina
RESIDENCE:	Davidson, North Carolina
JERSEY NO.:	20
POSITION:	Running back
HEIGHT:	5-foot-10
WEIGHT:	250 pounds

The Run-Up

Natrone Means arrived in San Diego in 1993, fresh from Tobacco Road.

Picked by then-general manager Bobby Beathard in the second round out of North Carolina, Means wasn't blue about being a Charger.

But he was hardly embraced in a running backs' room full of veterans.

"When I got there they had Marion Butts, Eric Bieniemy, and Ronnie Harmon," Means said. "They took [me] under their wing."

Really, Natrone?

"OK, Eric and Buttsy took me under their wing," Means said. "Ronnie made things tough on everyone.

"But after being there for a while and cutting my teeth with those guys, they were good. I was fortunate enough to come into that [running backs] room and work with those guys. They were business-first guys and I couldn't have been in a better room as a rookie in the NFL."

Finding space to run was where Means initially struggled. He still recalls his first carry in a rookie minicamp drill during his first NFL offseason.

"You know to be honest with you when I took the handoff I knew I was in a different place," Means said. "It was an inside zone run and I saw the damn hole right there in front of me.

"But by the time I got to that hole it was shut. I said, 'Wow, what happened to it?'

"What that told me was there wasn't going to be much dancing behind the line of scrimmage at this level. If you see a hole, you better get there fast."

Means paid his dues while playing second fiddle to Butts. Although Means validated Beathard's confidence in him after Means led the team with eight rushing touchdowns.

Among those scores—despite the fact that Means was built like a classic short-yardage back—was a 65-yard scamper.

But that year came with its share of head-scratching for Means.

"It was so different coming from college," he admitted. "I had no idea what to expect in the NFL, didn't have a clue.

"When the NFL guys came back and talked to us at college, they never talked about all the work you put in. They just talked about playing ball.

"So when I got to San Diego, it was an eye-opening experience. It was an adjustment, as I felt like I was a freshman in college again. It really took me a while to find my way."

But he had a head coach who was relatively fresh from a college campus as well. After leaving Georgia Tech, Bobby Ross was in his second year with the Chargers during Means's rookie year.

"Having Coach Ross not being too far removed from college himself, in a sense there were some similarities," Means said. "But really in the pros this is your job 24/7. Those are the things you learn to deal with in order to be successful. Coach Ross is a guy I remember being a strong man."

Means also recalls running backs coach Sylvester Croom. The old-school assistant with a baritone voice once lit into an unsuspecting Means.

"I remember my position coach said, 'Hey, you missed a lift this morning,'" Means said. "I said, 'Oh, I didn't know I had to lift weights if I didn't want to.' I thought you lifted weights if you just wanted to get stronger. I didn't know it was required.

"I had to do some growing up when I came to the NFL."

The Game

By Natrone Means

In trying to think about the game that means the most to me, I would think about that playoff game when we beat Miami in the 1994 season.

But then again, speaking in terms of which game really meant the most to me, honest to God, it was a game that we lost.

Even though we lost, it was one of the best games that I ever played in.

It was a 7–6 loss against the Raiders that we played up in Oakland.

I remember it because that day we only had 195 yards in total offense and I had 167 of those yards.

Man, our defense was balling out. But on offense we couldn't get anything going through the air [with quarterbacks Ryan Leaf and Craig Whelihan]. We were struggling in the air so on the ground we kept chipping and chipping away.

The reason that was the best game I played is just because it was the one game in my career, that after when it was all over, I was done for a week.

I mean I was done for a week because I couldn't walk. I actually couldn't practice until the walk-through the next Saturday when it was time to do it all over again on Sunday.

But after that game in Oakland, I definitely paid for it. I felt like they had put me in a burlap sack and beat my [tail].

It wasn't one guy on the Raiders. It was collective [butt] kicking. Those defenders were all over the place and all over me.

I remember that game because rushing-wise, I had 37 carries for 101 yards and those were tough yards to come by.

And I also caught six passes coming out of the backfield. So I had 101 rushing yards and 66 receiving yards.

I really felt like there was nothing else I could have done that day and that's why it is one of my favorite games even though we lost that game.

John Carney kicked two field goals and we were winning, 6–0. Our defense was playing lights out, just shutting the Raiders out the whole game.

We had Junior Seau, Rodney Harrison, John Parrella, guys like that. We had like the No. 1 defense in the league during that time and we were in the top five with our rushing game. But our air attack was terrible.

We were 2–4 after that loss [coach Kevin Gilbride was fired the following Tuesday].

The Raiders ended up scoring late in the game and they took a 7–6 lead. We had turned the ball over in the fourth quarter, but we held them. But later on they scored the game's only touchdown.

We got the ball back again in the final minute and were driving to get into field-goal range for Carney to kick another field goal to take a 9–7 lead.

I took a screen pass from the left side on fourth-and-7 at the Oakland 38-yard line. I caught that pass and I'm telling you I had one of the best juke moves of my life.

But they said I fell 1 yard short of the first down. I'm telling you, I got that damn first down. I got a bad spot from the official and we ended up losing 7–6. I will never forget that game because it was one of the best games I had ever played in my life.

And I will never forget that play—I had that first down!

Raiders defensive tackle Darrell Russell later told me I got that first down.

Man, those Raiders games were always tough. There are just certain teams that when you played that team, you knew the defense was tough. It was teams like the Pittsburgh Steelers, Houston Oilers, Baltimore Ravens, and Raiders.

You knew it was going to be tough and that year's Raiders team was no exception. And then with the game being in Oakland, there was all the madness going on in the stands with all the fights.

But that game . . . I wasn't a finesse guy weighing 250 pounds. So the more physical the game, the better for me. That was what I was used to and I liked to mix it up.

But I didn't prefer to get my [butt] beat. I came out of that so sore. It was like the worst week of my eight-year career. I could barely walk the next day as I felt like I had been assaulted because they beat the hell out of me. I couldn't jog until the next Friday. Then two days later, it was time to do it all over again.

The Aftermath

He was the youngest player to score a touchdown in a Super Bowl. He was the super player in an offense that was constructed to run the ball.

And after the 1995 season, he wasn't super surprised he was shown the door in San Diego.

Natrone Means of the San Diego Chargers became Natrone Means of the Jacksonville Jaguars, just two years after leading the franchise to its lone Super Bowl.

Leading up to the '95 campaign, Means skipped most of training camp and was fined for his transgression. Means, among the most popular Chargers, stared down general manager Beathard after pacing the team in rushing the previous two years.

"I have not reported until now because I have a very serious personal matter that still needs to be taken care of," Means said in a statement faxed to reporters. "I feel that I have been seriously betrayed by Bobby Beathard. The matter is so serious that I have been willing to pass up a $100,000 reporting bonus and be fined $4,000 per day.

"I am addressing this issue publicly because I want to make sure the correct story is heard and I am sure that Beathard will make a statement that I am receiving bad advice. I want to make clear that this is my decision."

Means's representatives had advised him to release that missive. Looking back it was a bad move, Means said.

"We wanted a new contract and we were holding out and the whole deal," Means said. "After that came out in the papers, I wish I had shut that down. But I was letting my agent take care of that and I was taking care of the football side of things. But that really damaged the relationship with me and the Chargers. It was the business side of the game."

Means discovered the business side of the waiver wire after an injury-marred season in which he rushed for a team-high 730 yards and five touchdowns. Despite being under contract, the Chargers cut the physical running back after both parties sustained bruised feelings.

"I had heard the grumblings so I can't really say I was completely surprised," Means said.

He signed with the Jaguars, but he was hurt again—that goes for his body and soul.

"That's true, but then I got to get back to work," he said. "I still got to eat."

But the toast of the town in San Diego didn't have the same cache in Jacksonville.

"The way that whole thing started down there was frustrating," Means said. "I had a good preseason; then I got hurt and I had to start all over again. They even had me playing special teams at one point. But we eventually won some games and [had] a good run in the playoffs. It turned out well."

So did Means and San Diego. Beathard made him a Charger again in 1998 when Means reunited with head coach Gilbride, his offensive coordinator in Jacksonville in 1996.

"It's always good to know that you are wanted back," said Means, whose No. 20 jersey remains a common sight on game days in San Diego. "I just wish I had been able to be a little more successful."

Means's second San Diego stint went from 1998–99. But really, he never left either of the times he said goodbye.

He was, and remains, a favorite and integral part of the 1994 Chargers, one of the greatest teams in franchise history. Means was named to its 50th anniversary team.

"I used to have fun in San Diego," Means said. "I didn't play the superstar role; that was never me. I tried to be nice to all the people there."

He was a punishing running back with a little kid's wide smile. Yes, Means meant business with the football. But with or without it, Means meant a lot to Chargers fans.

Chapter 16

DARREN BENNETT

Chargers at Raiders—September 3, 1995

BIRTH DATE:	January 9, 1965
HOMETOWN:	Sydney, Australia
RESIDENCE:	Carlsbad, California
JERSEY NO.:	2
POSITION:	Punter
HEIGHT:	6-foot-5
WEIGHT:	235 pounds

The Run-Up

Darren Bennett's journey to America's Finest City is almost as good as the Australian's stellar career.

Bennett was an Australian Rules Football League star when he won a kicking contest in 1993. The winner received a trip to the United States and Bennett used that as his honeymoon with his wife, Rosemary.

So Bennett landed in Seattle and started making calls. Not that many were returned.

Bennett had never punted a football, let alone played in an American football game.

But Bennett knew somebody who knew somebody else and they knew someone in the Chargers' front office. That eventually led to Bennett knocking on the door of Marty Hurney, then-general manager Bobby Beathard's top assistant.

Intrigued, Hurney took Bennett down to the Qualcomm Stadium turf. With the Chargers not practicing and no long snapper available, Bennett flipped a football in front of him. He unleashed a booming punt, and the legend from Down Under was born.

"I kicked a couple of them pretty good, mate," Bennett said.

Hurney couldn't contain his excitement and asked Bennett if he had auditioned for anyone else. Bennett said, "No," but two other teams were interested.

"How much, I didn't know," Bennett said. "But maybe it was good that they didn't know either."

Hurney summoned the easygoing Beathard, who Bennett didn't know from Jimmy Buffett.

"This guy comes down dressed like he's going to the beach," Bennett said. "Maybe that made me more relaxed."

Instead, Beathard got jittery.

"I think Bobby was worried I was going to sign with another team," Bennett said.

The Chargers told Bennett to return for practice the next day, where he lined up behind long snapper Sam Anno.

Anno fired back the football and Bennett's rugged face might still sport the mark where it bopped the unsuspecting Aussie.

"It went right through my hands," Bennett said. "I had never caught a football to punt before."

Bennett would recover and continue to impress. But saying he was raw was as obvious as Bennett's heavy accent.

He needed work—lots of it. But the Chargers knew they had a prospect. They introduced Bennett to special teams coach Chuck Priefer, gave him footballs for practice, told him to travel safely back to Australia, and instructed him to call Hurney after the Super Bowl.

"We got the Super Bowl on the TV in Melbourne and I'm watching Buffalo play the Dallas Cowboys," Bennett said. "So the day after the Super Bowl, I call the Chargers. Of course everyone is on vacation after the Super Bowl, but I didn't know that.

"I call a week later and there's still no Marty Hurney. So I said, 'Screw this' and I just got on a plane in Melbourne and flew over."

He entered the Chargers' offices and saw the warm smile of longtime receptionist Georgette Rogers.

"I say, 'Is Marty in? And she goes, 'Yes, he just got back in' and I said, 'Good, I'm Darren Bennett from Australia.'"

The next person to enter the lobby was Hurney, with a look of disbelief.

"Marty comes out and says, 'What are you doing here?'" Bennett said. "I said, 'You said to get in touch after the Super Bowl.'"

Hurney explained he meant deeper into the offseason. But when a guy travels the globe, it's hard to shoo him away.

"So Marty introduced me to Chuck again and Chuck and I made a plan," Bennett said.

Bennett retreated with videos and footballs tucked under his arm. He returned for the 1994 training camp and found company.

"That was the year they were maybe looking to change from John Kidd so we had four punters," Bennett said.

"We had Sean Snyder, [University of Kansas football coach] Bill Snyder's kid, Scott McCallister, and this other guy, Kent Sullivan, and Kent had been in camp for a month and a half. Kent thought I was a long snapper because I was so big.

"He said, 'What do you do?' I said, 'I came here to punt for the San Diego Chargers.'"

Though that didn't seem to go over well with Sullivan, Bennett decided to let their play dictate who got the job.

"I go, 'Really? Let's go on the field and see.' He got my hackles up right away."

When Bennett put his feet up, home was a nearby hotel where he stayed with another punter seeking work, Mike Hollis.

"[Hollis] went off to Jacksonville and played for 10 years," Bennett said. "I remember those years at the Town & Country Hotel, jumping in the pool, drinking beer, and talking about what we were going to do.

"I was very naive. I was just there for the experience rather than anything else. I think that maybe helped me, too."

What hurt was Bennett being summoned into coach Bobby Ross's office at the end of camp. Bennett had made the team, but as a practice squad member.

"I went in and said, 'Coach, I'm twenty-nine years old. I'm too old to be on the practice squad. I've had a whole career back in Australia and you're really going to put me on the practice squad?'

"He said, 'Look, when I was at Kansas City we had a thirty-nine-year-old kicker and a forty-year-old punter. You got 10 years to do this if you get it right.'"

Bennett was blessed.

That 1994 team was the only Chargers squad to advance to the Super Bowl. If Bennett, as a rookie, had struggled early he might have been cut and forgotten.

"I didn't know what the hell I was doing," Bennett admitted. "I didn't want to be the guy to screw all this up. They might have given me the job and pulled the hook really quick."

Instead Bennett and the coaches built a trust without him trying to build his resume. When he became the punter in 1995, there was a comfort level between the parties that had been forged over a year and a half.

Of course the main reason Bennett was petrified about being cut didn't pertain to his teammates.

"I would get deported," he said. "I had a very specific athletic visa to play football for the San Diego Chargers, so that was part of my motivation.

"I used to say to these guys that 'If you get cut you can go back to Kansas or Texas. I've got to go back to Australia and none of these guys know how to dial that number back to Australia.' I think I put that pressure on myself on purpose, just for the motivation."

From Melbourne to Mission Valley, Bennett made it.

"Rosemary and I, we call it our big adventure," Bennett said. "And it was like that, from week to week, for probably two or three years."

The Game

By Darren Bennett

My first game was memorable to me because it had been a two-year process: the practice squad, a year of practice, NFL Europe, and just the fact it was the Raiders and they had moved back to Oakland.

It was huge. The energy was huge. The Raiders fans were trying to show everyone how happy they were to have them back.

My first game was the Raiders' very first game back in Oakland.

I knew about the Raiders' mystique and I'm panicking because it is my very first game. And [special teams coach] Chuck Priefer was panicking about Albert Lewis, who was the best punt-blocker in the NFL at the time.

And I'm punting to Tim Brown.

So nowadays I look back at those guys as legends of the game. But at the time, they were just the scariest guys playing.

It wasn't a great punting game for me. I think I averaged 40-something yards—along the ground. I'm not sure I had any hang time.

My get-off was so fast because all I did was watch Albert Lewis.

But I think it built the foundation for the rest of that year. I felt like after that first week, I didn't get one blocked, I didn't give up a big return.

I can't remember if we won. [Oakland prevailed, 17–7].

But it was my first game in the NFL. So that was a significant game for me.

You notice the Black Hole in pregame and Al Davis is walking around in his jump suit. But for me the crowds never played into it in any of my games. Even though once in Oakland they were throwing coins at me when we were under the uprights.

It's madness. The thing about the Oakland fans is they will read the media guide. They will be sitting there and say, "Where is so and so?" Or that they met my wife in a hotel last night and did nasty things.

They would pee in cups and throw it at you. They would do all sorts of stuff like that.

We used to get that in Australia, too. There was a team called Collingwood in Melbourne; they are the Raiders of Aussie Rules.

But it was just the combination of punting to Tim Brown and having Albert Lewis trying to get close to my punts. It was a like sense of achievement at the end of the day. Like, "OK I didn't get fired today—maybe I will get another game next week."

There were a couple of punts that Albert Lewis got close. Albert was always close. He had these big, long arms and his hand was always waving across the punter, trying to get a hand on the ball.

He was one of those guys on punt return that you need to know where he was at any stage.

But on the first couple they backed off because they didn't know how I was going to punt.

They had no film on me really. I think they were trying to set up a return.

Tim Brown got no returns because the [punts] rolled along on the ground; Chuck said that was horrible.

Maybe I was ahead of myself, as they do punts on the ground nowadays.

I was killing worms. In fact, the closest anyone came to blocking one was probably my guy's helmet in front of me because the [punts] weren't going very high in the air.

But it was effective and you think you'll get another week out of it. No big returns!

I was in survival mode, I really was. The preseason to the regular season, the pressure ramps up, and then the playoffs, it does it again.

So I had had two preseason games and sort of felt like I knew what I was doing and in control a little bit of my punting. But there was a lot of pressure.

I had no idea about the rest of the game going on around me.

So I had felt like I coped with that pressure, not greatly, just that I had. So it kind of gave me a little bit of confidence.

The Aftermath

Darren Bennett, a two-time Pro Bowler, more than survived his first and most memorable game. He went on to an eleven-year career that had a significant impact on and off the field.

Although every punter is only as good as his last effort.

"Even after my first Pro Bowl they would bring someone in against me in training camp and you go, 'I'm only two of three shanks away from getting waved goodbye,'" he said.

But really for Bennett it was mostly no worries, mate.

With his knack for booming kicks, Bennett could flip the field position in a heartbeat.

But it was his touch, his precision, that ability to make a football check up like a golf ball on an approach shot that separated him. It was his ability to keep punts from bouncing into the end zone for touchbacks that became Bennett's forte.

By kicking the ball just right, he could make it land in the wrong spot for opposing offenses. Now every NFL, and most college punters, has that weapon in their arsenal.

It was an Aussie Rules kick that Bennett let tag along from Down Under.

While Bennett's accurate punts put a damper on returns, he was showered with awards.

He was selected to the NFL's 1990 All-Decade team.

Twice he was selected All-Pro and was a two-time Pro Bowler.

That's more than a g'day, mate. That's a good career and one that landed him in the Chargers Hall of Fame.

To think Bennett went from nearly having his nose broken by a firm snap to being among the game's best is amazing.

"I still don't know why I made those things, but it was a tremendous honor to be an Australian who had never played the game and five years later you are on the All-1990s team," said Bennett, who had a 43.4-yard career average.

Bennett's accomplishments are impressive. But in a clear display of his Aussie humor, there's one achievement that Bennett holds higher above all others.

"I think the best one I ever made was the All-Madden team," Bennett said, setting up his punch line. "I beat out the Budweiser horse."

Say again?

"The year before they said there was no decent specialist after Steve Tasker [of the Buffalo Bills] retired," Bennett said. "So they put the Budweiser horse on it, the Clydesdale horse kicking a field goal in the commercial. That was Madden's special-teamer, like a tongue-in-cheek thing.

"So to be the special-teams guy a year after that is special because, well, I beat out a horse."

Aussie punters beat a path to Bennett's home in the northern San Diego County city of Carlsbad. He not only coaches them, but Rosemary gleefully cooks some Aussie grub and smiles follow.

A big grin is also Bennett's reaction when mentioning what he's done for young Aussie players with an eye on America.

"Being in the NFL, that's a one-in-a-million shot," Bennett said. "But you can send these kids to colleges and they can develop skills there. They are getting scholarships, degrees, and having an American college experience."

Those Aussies aren't only at home with Bennett. Their approach, which was introduced by Bennett, is the rage regardless of nationality.

"They all roll out now and punt," Bennett said. "They're playing Aussie Rules, basically, on an American field. It looks ugly and it's not a spiral, but it works."

Bennett transformed from being a work-in-progress to helping other Aussies find work—and schools—in the good ol' US of A.

"You take pride in that," he said. "Someone had to be first, but I didn't feel like a trailblazer at the time. I just felt nervous and was trying not to lose a job. I never thought of how long it was going to go on."

Chapter 17

DENNIS GIBSON

Chargers at Steelers—January 15, 1995

BIRTH DATE:	February 8, 1964
HOMETOWN:	Des Moines, Iowa
RESIDENCE:	Ankeny, Iowa
JERSEY NO.:	57
POSITION:	Linebacker
HEIGHT:	6-foot-2
WEIGHT:	240 pounds

The Run-up

Dennis Gibson loved playing for the Detroit Lions. It was the team that drafted him and where he established himself as a steady, if not spectacular, player over seven seasons.

Even after reaching free agency in 1994, he wanted to return to the Motor City, and the Lions were revved to keep him.

Then again . . .

"When I became a free agent my agent said San Diego wanted me to come out and take a visit," Gibson said. "I didn't know much about San Diego."

What he was familiar with were teams built by Bobby Beathard. The Chargers' general manager was building a roster for his fourth season with the Chargers, after working his magic for years with the Washington Redskins.

Gibson knew all about the Redskins after battling them numerous times while playing for the Lions. His respect for Beathard's handiwork eclipsed his lack of knowledge of San Diego's blueprint.

"The big thing for me was Bobby Beathard," Gibson said. "His Washington Redskins teams, with Joe Gibbs as coach, had the reputation of making wise personnel moves. And that was really before free agency. But he made moves by drafting the right guys and putting players together that won championships."

But Gibson, who played at Iowa State, was a Midwest guy and at ease in Detroit.

"It probably was the hardest decision I ever made," Gibson said. "I loved Detroit. I was in the same defense with the same guys for seven years. I was just really comfortable there. I knew what I was doing and knew our schemes inside and out because I had done it so long.

"But the thing that made me want to come to San Diego was Beathard."

Gibson could sense his career winding down. He figured if Beathard could construct Super Bowl teams on the East Coast there was no reason he couldn't do it on the opposite coast. But there was no guarantee the Chargers would get there, or that Gibson would be around, if they did.

"I was in my eighth year so it could have been one-and-done when I got there," he said. "You never know what is going to happen. But everyone wants to get to that game, the Super Bowl. Anybody who plays football for a profession thinks of that.

"We had got to the playoffs with the Lions but we would lose. One of those losses was to the Redskins."

So Gibson rolled the dice.

"Every player wants to win a world championship and for me I thought this was my best opportunity," he said. "But the Lions wanted me to come back. It was hard not to go back. But this was what I had to do."

Wise decision? Gibson wasn't sure during offseason workouts at UC San Diego.

"When I first got there, to training camp, I had to work so hard to learn new schemes, learn about new coaches, and learn this new city," Gibson said. "Unfortunately with all those things, after a couple of weeks of camp, my attitude was, 'What were you thinking?' I was second-guessing myself."

Then Gibson had a team meeting—with just himself.

"I thought, *Hey, this is your decision you made to give yourself the best chance to get to a Super Bowl. So quit thinking about it.* But in hindsight, I wasn't sure about it."

Gibson eventually found his San Diego legs, fitting in on a defense that featured Junior Seau, Leslie O'Neal, Chris Mims, Raylee Johnson, and a special teams player who got occasional action on passing downs—Rodney Harrison.

"I was really fortunate that I took that shot by going to San Diego," said Gibson, who played just two years with the Chargers. "It might not have worked out for me, but it fell into place."

That was especially true in the 1994 AFC Championship Game. Gibson's deflection of a fourth-down pass clinched the win for the Chargers against the Pittsburgh Steelers, advancing San Diego to its lone Super Bowl.

A painting of Gibson's iconic play hangs prominently in the reception area at Chargers Park.

"Of all the guys, Gibson," Beathard said, chuckling with the irony. "He wasn't the fastest guy, wasn't very quick, and pass coverage was his weakness. But he was smart."

At the very least, he was keen enough to know that San Diego was the place he ought to be.

The Game

By Dennis Gibson

I know in Pittsburgh it was a foregone conclusion they were punching their ticket to go to the Super Bowl. I don't think that helped them as they kind of put the cart before the horse.

We had started the season hot but cooled off in the second half. But we were confident if we stayed relatively healthy and

we played our game that we could have a reasonable shot in the playoffs.

We didn't want to let them run the ball. We wanted to try and have them beat us through the air, that was our game plan—that was the whole deal.

Typically that was the game plan every week because in those days the running game was more dominant. Almost everyone was running schemes like that and there was so much play-action, misdirection, bootleg-type runs. Any time a team is running the ball against you, the play-action will kill you.

We played a lot of zone and on the play-action the linebackers get sucked up on the play, thinking it is a run. Then they find the void between you and in the secondary, right over [the] top of the line in the middle area. They had the right guys to pass the ball to in the middle of the field.

As much as the game has changed a lot since then, it is still the same: the good teams run the ball.

If we played great defense and controlled the game with our offense a little, we would be OK. If we had to punt sometimes and play defense to get some field position, that was fine.

They were winning 10–3 at halftime but there wasn't any panic; the game was not out of reach. We figured with two scores we had a chance to win the game. We made some adjustments at halftime and sat down and talked to the coaches. They knew what the Steelers were doing to hurt us and what they were going to try and do.

One thing about [defensive coordinator] Bill Arnsparger is he kept it simple. I played on some defenses that were pretty good in the league, in San Diego and in Detroit, and the best ones always had the simplest schemes. That gave you the ability to react no matter what you see. You play with great confidence, with the coaches just giving you the rules to play by.

If they do this, you do that, no matter what formation they put out there or what personnel. Just follow the rules and you can play the game without thinking about it.

You get in trouble when you are scratching your head out there. But with Bill, he kept it simple.

I remember the big play [a fourth-quarter Stan Humphries to Tony Martin 43-yard touchdown pass to put the Chargers ahead, 17–13], but in terms of seeing what happened, I couldn't tell you. When the other side of the ball, the offense, has the ball, you are sitting on the bench trying to figure what you have to do to get the game won.

They get the ball back with five minutes left and they have 65, 70 yards to go. We didn't want to give up any big chunks, make them go 10–15 plays. Then I bit on an out route to one of the tight ends [Eric Green] and he found the seam. I said, "OK, maybe it's time to start taking some chances" because it was getting toward the end of the game and we couldn't let that happen again. We could feel it slipping away and we knew if we didn't do something . . . we got in the huddle and said, "Who is going to make the play to turn this thing around?"

One of the most vivid memories of that game, after they go over midfield in our territory at about the 30-, 35-yard line, was Junior Seau going berserk. He was out of his mind, just yelling and I can't tell what he is saying. They are already lined up for the play and he is still on my side of the ball. I grab him and push him over to the other side.

I'm like, "No man, over here, over here!" It's a lot different for me because I was playing middle linebacker and getting the call in is huge. So your attention is on the sidelines, looking at Arnsparger to find out what front and coverage we are going to run.

Then I look back and Junior is running around in a frenzy.

Bill was the calmest dude I ever met. Bobby [Ross] was going berserk, everyone was yelling, it was pure pandemonium.

Junior was beside himself; he saw it slipping away. But I had to get everyone lined up in the right defense and I was yelling and screaming at Junior, but he couldn't hear me. So I just grabbed him and pushed him over to where he needed to be. He was really excited, but I guess we all were.

They stayed in their regular personnel on the drive, two tight ends. We didn't bring in a nickelback; they were running the ball successfully and the whole series we went with the same base personnel.

The Steelers fans were being quiet in between plays as they kept moving the ball down the field. It almost felt inevitable that they were going to punch that thing in and it would be back to the Super Bowl for what had been a long time for the Pittsburgh Steelers.

Everything is going though your head. If we can just keep them out, this game is over and we are going to the Super Bowl.

On first down at the nine, they ran a draw with John Parrella tackling Barry Foster for a loss.

Then a couple of plays before the fourth-down play, I expected them to run that route to the tight end, Green, again. Basically he would move inside on the linebacker and then push off on the outside. They did it and I was able to get my hands on it but I didn't make the interception.

That's when I was thinking that chance is not going to happen again. I blew it. You just had your opportunity to end the game and you didn't get done—you idiot! You just don't get that many opportunities.

They get a pass for seven yards on third down and are down to the three.

But the thing about them getting closer to the end zone is it gets easier to play defense. The closer to [the] end zone they are, their options become limited. The defense just had to back up a step into the end zone and make sure everything stays in front of you.

On the fourth-down play they were in the shotgun and the receivers on the outside were covered up. Neil O'Donnell checked down to Foster and was looking at him all the way.

O'Donnell looked him down the whole way and I was able to get around and knock the ball down with my left hand. I broke on it so fast, before he threw it, that Foster didn't have a chance to catch it.

When you look back at it, you swear to God it is all in slow motion. You know he is going to throw it to him, but you are running in place and not getting there, that is the nightmare.

The amazing part about it, and one of the biggest things you remember from that game, was you couldn't believe how instantly that many people could be quiet.

To this day, people ask me about that play.

The Aftermath

Hard to match an occupation that sends an NFL team to its first, and only, Super Bowl.

For a second act, Dennis Gibson currently flips pies at Encore Pizza.

Makes sense, no?

Gibson would play just one more season in the NFL after he prevented the Pittsburgh Steelers' Barry Foster from catching a potential go-ahead touchdown pass in the 1994 AFC Championship Game's waning moments. Gibson's second season with the Chargers the following year was his last as a professional. His 69 tackles were fifth-best on a Chargers team that was bounced by the Jim Harbaugh-led Colts in an AFC Wild Card Game.

The defending AFC champions were done and so was Gibson.

His pizza joint is usually jumping and it seems that indelible mark in Chargers history is a constant, like the aroma of marinara sauce.

"People ask me about the three things that I most remember about it," Gibson said. "It's meeting my parents after the game, having to grab Junior Seau to get him in the right place, and the fourth-down play. People are still talking about it all these years later."

It put the Chargers in the Super Bowl and on the occasion of the NFL's 50th Super Bowl, something special happened to Gibson.

To honor the game's golden anniversary, Super Bowl participants went back to their high schools. The player then presented the school with a special gold NFL Super Bowl football, to mark his accomplishment of being in a special, or some say, super-athletic fraternity.

Gibson, his wife, and their four children took center court at halftime of an Ankeny High School boys basketball game. The play that made Gibson famous to Chargers fans came alive again, to a new generation.

Better yet, Gibson, who lives but two miles from the school, got to share this with his family.

"I gave my gold football to the athletic director and the principal," Gibson said. "It was cool."

Things have changed in Ankeny since Gibson was a star there, beginning a football career that would include one of the most memorable moments in Chargers history. His old coach now works across town at Centennial High School and Gibson's hometown grows bigger. But his memorable play never diminishes.

"My hometown has changed because in those days there was just one high school," he said. "They split the enrollment in half and now there are two high schools. But still, there's nothing like going back to your old high school.

"A lot of people thought it was neat and I received a lot of notes on social media. My wife kind of handles that and she posted a picture of us with our four kids at halftime.

"My oldest kid didn't want to go out there. But my wife said you're going out there for the picture."

The snapshot of the 1994 Chargers is etched in Gibson's mind. The team had stars, and to be frank, Gibson wasn't one of them.

"I was just one of the guys on the team," he said. "But that was one of the reasons we were so successful. Everybody had a role and great teams know that you need everyone to know what they are supposed to. Coach [Bobby] Ross, he was the guy that understood that."

Gibson's great moment breathed again at a prep basketball game in America's heartland. The NFL had a super idea with the Super Bowl alumni program and that was crystal clear on a chilly night in Ankeny, Iowa.

"I've been away from it for so long," Gibson said. "But it was a time to reflect on what we did. We didn't win the Super Bowl, but getting there was still a huge deal. It's one of those feel-good things.

"And it's just amazing that people still ask me about it all these years later."

Chapter 18

CRAIG WHELIHAN

Chiefs at Chargers—November 22, 1998

BIRTH DATE:	April 15, 1971
HOMETOWN:	San Jose, California
RESIDENCE:	Cardiff, California
JERSEY NO.:	5
POSITION:	Quarterback
HEIGHT:	6-foot-0
WEIGHT:	205 pounds

The Run-up

Craig Whelihan, if nothing else, was well-rested when he saw his first NFL action.

A sixth-round pick in 1995, Whelihan finally trotted onto the field in Week 8 of the 1997 season. He was thrilled, even though his role was that of a mop-up man in a 31–3 loss to the Chiefs.

With starter Stan Humphries continually being hampered by concussions, Whelihan started the Chargers' final seven games. With losses in each of those outings, Whelihan was the closest thing the Chargers had to James Bond. San Diego sportswriters tagged him "007," even if he was one zero shy.

Behind a leaky offensive line Whelihan was shaken and stirred during his stint in the '97 season's second half. He looked to 1998 as a fresh start, buoyed by the fact that he played, even if he didn't win.

"I heard everything before the draft that the Chargers were trying to decide between Peyton Manning and Ryan Leaf," Whelihan said. "But at the minicamp practices I was feeling really good and running with the first team.

"All through the offseason I thought I could compete with anyone, even if they brought in a veteran. I had started those games and was confident."

But the Chargers, coming off a 4–12 season, were just as certain Leaf was the team's savior. He arrived with a strong right arm and a dose of hype as the second overall pick to match it.

Many thought the Chargers would add an experienced quarterback to complement Leaf and Whelihan. Coach Kevin Gilbride, who lasted but six games that season, four of which were losses, before being fired, pleaded with general manager Bobby Beathard to sign Warren Moon.

The Chargers, instead, thought they had a star in Leaf.

Whelihan incorrectly felt he had a shot to be number one.

"I was still running the reps with the starters through most of training camp," Whelihan said. "Then we had FanFest Day at Qualcomm Stadium and had a scrimmage. At that point, Kevin made the switch to Ryan. It wasn't communicated or anything, it just happened.

"Look, I knew when they brought Ryan in and invested that much money in him—he was making millions and I was making maybe a third of that—I realized the writing was on the wall. But I was going to do everything possible not to lose my job."

Instead, Leaf lost his grip on what it meant to be a professional.

While the overachieving Whelihan begged to be recognized, the Chargers looked the other way regarding Leaf's questionable behavior.

The turnovers mounted from Leaf and the tumultuous nature of his antics weighed on the fractured locker room. It was clear Leaf wanted to be a star. And it was just as obvious he didn't want to put in the work to allow just that.

"That was the tough part," Whelihan said. "He didn't prepare. He was the last guy to show up and the first guy to leave and it was frustrating to me because I wanted to scream and yell and say, 'Why is this happening? Can you not see that I'm putting in the work?'"

But the snaps kept going to Leaf, especially after the Chargers defeated the Buffalo Bills and Tennessee Oilers to open the season. Leaf would continue to play, even after the team lost six out of the next seven games.

"I came from the old school where a rookie has to sit on the pine and learn," Whelihan said. "It wasn't like I was a free agent looking to play. I was drafted, too, although it was five rounds after Leaf. But everyone has to sit and learn, even Tom Brady did that. I just wanted that job so badly and he didn't really want to be the starting quarterback. I remember when they finally put me in he was the biggest cheerleader on the sidelines. He was so relieved not to be in there.

"Look, I'm not going to sit here some 20 years later and talk bad about Ryan. But the fact was he was always going to Las Vegas and doing all the other stuff. I knew I had to be ready at any point because as he started to struggle, you could see it was going to be a tough road for him."

The Game

By Craig Welihan

There were two games in 1998 that I think about as the games of my life. That was the year of Ryan Leaf and they came after coach Kevin Gilbride got let go.

I beat Baltimore but I just felt like I managed the game. I had to just not turn the ball over and not screw it up.

But in the Kansas City game, we came back after being down by 17 points in the fourth quarter to win, 38–37. That was the game where I had to go out and make plays.

Natrone Means was hurt, so we didn't have him. But we had like the number one defense with guys like Junior Seau, Kurt Gouveia, Rodney Harrison, John Parrella, Raylee Johnson; the defense was just stacked. And we were killing them just rushing the ball. Natrone was out but we had Terrell Fletcher and Tremayne Stephens and Kenny Bynum. We were playing a ball-control game with no turnovers. I just wanted to make good throws, be accurate, and not turn the ball over.

We were leading, 17–14, at halftime and our locker room was really fired up and excited. Coach June Jones told me we are going to attack them right away. We were going to go over the top. Do a play-action and get over the top.

I was going for Ryan Thelwell and needless to say I didn't see the free safety, Jerome Woods. It was my fault it was underthrown; I did not put a lot of air on it. I turned it over and they went down and scored to make it 21–17.

Then Latario Rachal turned the ball over on a punt for our second turnover in the third quarter and they [kicked] a field goal to make it 24–17.

I remember thinking during that quarter, let's not start this, making mistakes. But then again, after we got the ball back, I scrambled up into the pocket, not trying to buy time but trying to make yardage and I got hit by one of the defensive linemen and Chester McClockton recovered it.

So that's three turnovers in the third quarter and they go up 24–17.

Then early in the fourth quarter, they go up by 17 points, 34–17.

That was when June just turned to me and said, "We are going to the two-minute drill the whole quarter. We're not going to huddle, get in and out as fast as you can and just get to the line of scrimmage quickly."

I thought, *Hey, whatever we have to do at this point.* It's no longer let's play it safe; whatever the next play is that's what we were thinking. It wasn't about not turning it over. It was just the next play and just executing it.

We do a couple check downs, run it a couple of times and get it down to about their 10-yard line. I see Freddie Jones coming over the middle and then we got very fortunate. I threw the ball and it got blocked at the line of scrimmage and landed in Freddie Jones's hands for a first down. I said, "Thank you, thank you." Because at that point we had to score if we wanted to win the ball game and the fact it landed in Freddie's hands [and] got us a first down was huge. We then gave it to Terrell Fletcher for a touchdown and we're down by 10. But Kansas City kicks a field goal to go up by 13. Now we know we have to score two touchdowns.

On the next drive June tells me we're running four streaks down the field every time. Just look off a safety and pick which way you want to go and just unload it. I hit Thelwell for 55 yards and on fourth-and-13 we go for it and I went down the middle for Freddie Jones. He was wide open on a seam route off a post, caught it at the two, got hit at the one, and just walked in so we cut it to six points.

Kansas City gets the ball and it drives down in position to kick a field goal with 57 seconds left. If they make it, the game is over. They kick it and miss it. We've got no timeouts and we're down to our last drive.

But I felt like luck was on my side; for whatever reason things were going my way.

The drive starts and we do a check-down to Terrell Fletcher for 35 yards and he gets us to midfield. Then I throw an incomplete. We go for Mikhael Ricks downfield and James Hasty gets called for pass interference—a huge call.

We get to the 13 and I have two incompletes and have to clock it once. On fourth-and-10 from the 13 I go to Ricks again and Hasty is called again for pass interference to put it on the one with 16 seconds left.

On first down I threw a fade right to Ricks and he catches it but Reggie Tongue gets his hand in there as he is coming down: incomplete.

So now we call what everyone now calls a pick play.

Freddie Jones and Charlie Jones are on the right side and Freddie goes straight up the field and Charlie goes with him then goes across the end zone. I threw it off my back foot and it was on his back shoulder, behind him. He reaches back and pulls it in with his left hand.

I thought we had pulled to within one point; I didn't know we tied it. Then when John Carney kicked the extra point and they put 38–37 on the scoreboard I thought we might just have won this.

It was the moment of my career, being a third-string guy that was trying to find his way. Even though I was drafted, I was always behind Stan Humphries, Jim Everett, Sean Salisbury, Ryan Leaf. I was never the guy.

Then to go into the players' parking lot and see my dad, after he had come back from his stroke during the offseason. I was just sobbing and gave him a hug. Those were happy tears.

It was a moment you dream about and going back to Pop Warner, high school, college, pros, that was my most exciting game. And it came with a nice lesson: you actually can come back, and I proved it with a moment like that.

The Aftermath

Craig Whelihan stayed in football even after being cut by the Chargers following the 1999 preseason. Nevertheless, his connection in the NFL would be brief, as the Oakland Raiders kicked his tires during training camp in 2000, but little else. He didn't make it to opening day, but still he wouldn't deflate his dream of completing passes as a pro.

He spent time coaching at La Costa Canyon High, a school known for its powerhouse football teams in North San Diego County.

Whelihan subsequently saw action with the AFL—the Arena Football League—on three different teams.

Then there was a stint back in San Diego with af2—arena football 2—although Whelihan never threw a pass.

He found his way to his native San Jose with a return trip to the AFL. As a backup, he was part of the SaberCats' 2007 championship team.

After that, Whelihan was finished taking snaps. So he slapped on a referee's whistle.

"I was done with [playing] football, but I was obviously looking to stay in football," he said.

Even if it came with salty language whenever a coach thought he was done wrong.

"It's amazing to me that once you put on the official's uniform, immediately you are the enemy," he said. "That's the immediate reaction from fans and coaches. It's, 'You better make calls for us. Don't screw it up.'

"It's like, 'Hey, I'm here to help you play the game. Just worry about your game and don't think about mine.'"

The ex-NFL quarterback started at the game's lowest levels. On Saturdays, Whelihan works up to four games, ruling contests for kids who come up no higher than his waist.

"Being a Pop Warner referee is not awesome," Whelihan said. "A lot of dads think they know the rules."

Many don't recognize Whelihan and end up questioning his knowledge of the game's regulations and nuances.

"I'm tempted sometimes to say, 'Can I show you my resume?' I really do know the game a little bit," Whelihan said with a smile.

But Saturdays are only the end of a busy four-day run each week during football season.

He's keeping track of high school games before that, working the freshmen games on Thursdays, junior varsity on Friday afternoons, and then the varsity squads under the Friday night lights.

"It puts me right back in the decision-making," he said. "Every play you are in it, and that's offense and defense.

"When I was playing, whether you are on offense or defense, you get to go sit down when you're not on the field. When you are the referee, it doesn't matter, you have to ref it. And you have to ref the special teams, too."

Whelihan, who aspires to work in the Pac-12 and NFL, is earning his referee stripes as a line judge. That puts him within earshot of coaches.

"I like to be on the sidelines because the coaches are right there and they are giving it to me," he said. "And they complain to me about the other guys. The umpire, back judge, referee, they pretty much get to stay in the middle of [the] field. But when you're on the sidelines, they are letting you have it. They tell me I stink and then after a while I say, 'Come on coach.' They may not agree with me but the play goes on."

On occasion Whelihan referees with a former teammate. Moses Moreno, another former Chargers quarterback, is also a member of the San Diego County Referees Association.

"We have a blast because he is working the line, too," Whelihan said. "So we are working straight across from each other.

"It's just a lot of fun. It's like being part of a team again, the camaraderie and going through the game and trying to be perfect with all my calls. You get to hear the crunch of bodies on the line and you hear the competitiveness of the players and coaches. It's like you are right back in it."

Often, a coach takes Whelihan right back to the game of his life.

"To this day people remember that fourth quarter when we came back to beat Kansas City," he said. "They will say, 'Is that Whelihan?' And when they say that, I get immediate respect."

Chapter 19

LADAINIAN TOMLINSON

Broncos at Chargers—December 10, 2006

BIRTH DATE:	June 23, 1979
HOMETOWN:	Waco, Texas
RESIDENCE:	Fort Worth, Texas
JERSEY NO.:	21
POSITION:	Running back
HEIGHT:	5-foot-10
WEIGHT:	215 pounds

The Run-up

LaDainian Tomlinson entered Chargers Park in 2001 with his shoulders straight back.

Good thing, because a lot was riding on them.

Few Chargers experienced the highs and lows as much as Tomlinson did. He arrived as a first-round pick to save the day and he did, leading the Chargers on one of their most impressive runs in franchise history.

What makes Tomlinson's perspective so keen was that he, appropriately, got in on the ground floor.

"It was the building of the organization, the foundation that was set in place early on," he said.

"When I got here, the previous year they were 1–15. But walking into the locker room, Junior Seau and Rodney Harrison are present—guys that have played at a high level and had been leaders of teams."

Tomlinson was learning from the two Chargers greats on how to conduct his business. It was guidance that Tomlinson, unlike defenders, never stiff-armed.

"Just to watch them and learn how it was done, on and off the field, in practice, after practice in the film room . . . That really had an impact on me," he said.

The Chargers were soon on NFL highlight reels, thanks to Tomlinson's shifty feet. He supplied the leg work as general manager John Butler got busy.

"That foundation was set," Tomlinson said. "When we acquired more players in the draft and free agency, you could see we were building something special."

The fact that Tomlinson ended up in San Diego was shocking.

The Chargers had the first overall pick in 2001 and all signs pointed to them taking Virginia Tech quarterback Michael Vick. He was the consensus number one selection and some thought the football gods were finally blessing the Chargers.

The question was whether Vick's availability could be payback for the fallout from the last time the Chargers took a quarterback in the first round: Ryan Leaf in 1998.

But on the eve of the draft, Butler orchestrated a blockbuster trade.

The number one selection, aka Vick, was peddled to Atlanta, with the Falcons returning a package that included the fifth-overall pick.

With it the Chargers took Tomlinson, fresh from setting rushing records at Texas Christian University.

But there were growing pains.

The Chargers won 13 games in Tomlinson's first two seasons. In his third year, they won just four.

Meanwhile, he was producing three straight 1,000-yard seasons.

Then 4–12 became 12–4 and the Chargers won the AFC West in 2004.

But when the next season didn't include a playoff trip, some big changes took place. Among them was Philip Rivers supplanting Drew Brees at quarterback.

But Tomlinson remained the team's heart and soul, which helped produce the magic in 2006.

The Game

By LaDainian Tomlinson

It would have to be the touchdown record game against Denver. That was a very special moment. We never won a championship,

well a Super Bowl championship, I mean. We won a lot of championships.

But the one thing I remember [Coach] Marty [Schottenheimer] saying to me is that you had a lot of championship moments and breaking that record, with the fans and your teammates, that was a championship moment. Being at home and having my family in the stands and doing it behind our home crowd and the chants of "L. T., L. T."

I went into that game not really thinking I would get three touchdowns. Things have to go right for you to get three touchdowns obviously.

But I think I scored early in the first quarter so I knew this could be a pretty good game for us. Because usually when you take a while to score it is usually going to be tough sledding, if you don't score in the first quarter.

But if you get out to a good start and score early you know you are going to have other opportunities to score.

I remember I thought after the second one, I thought that was pretty much it. I was thinking, *Man, we probably won't get the ball back with enough time to go down and score.* But if you remember the big turnover happened, the sack fumble, and sure enough my linemen at the time said, "Let's go get the record." Everyone jumped off the bench and we ran back into the game.

I remember Kris Dielman, right before the play, looking right at me, and [he] said, "Follow me, follow me and we're going to get the record."

I followed him but [fullback] Lorenzo Neal fell down. So I just booked it to the sideline.

The play, "50 Power," that is supposed to go right behind Dielman. Once I see Lorenzo fall down, there was a defender there.

And they knew that we were probably going to run power, so they jammed it up inside.

Once I didn't see anything inside, I knew I had the defensive end to work with and the secondary, the late Darrent Williams, I had him to work with as well and I like my chances against a corner.

Coach Schottenheimer always said [that if] you let a cornerback tackle you, you don't belong in the league.

Once I got past that first guy, I kind of peaked inside and I knew [Williams] was too far away to get me before I could get to the end zone.

You don't really hear much during the play. But man, once I crossed the pylon, it erupted and I heard everything.

Teammates were running over, and I saw a lot of celebrations on the sidelines: coaching staff, front-office staff, business people.

That's why I say it was a championship moment. I envisioned when you win a Super Bowl championship that is what it would be like.

It was really a great moment.

I was emotional. Because I knew that we just did something that was special that had a chance to be around a long time. That's a lot of touchdowns, you know. A lot of stuff has to go right.

I wasn't expecting it [to be hoisted on his teammates' shoulders]. Your teammates, man, they tell the true story sometimes on how they feel about a player. To be lifted up like that? I felt the love from my teammates and I feel like they appreciated what just happened.

That is important. Imagine if we break that record and then I turn around and everyone is walking to the sidelines and I'm like, "Where is everybody?"

It would be a lonely feeling like, OK, thank you.

It was really a good moment for them to do that.

I was going to hug the first person I saw. So when I turned around I just had my arm out like whoever was running over to me they were going to get a big hug.

I just remember the offensive linemen wanted it as bad as I did.

We did something special. I told them at that time, this is something that when we are old, gray, and fat, which we are all getting there, that this is something we are going to remember.

The Aftermath

A stellar 14–2 season accompanied Tomlinson's 2006 NFL MVP campaign. The Chargers, relishing the "Marty Ball" approach their coach, Marty Schottenheimer preached, dominated the regular season in winning their final 10 games.

It was a run spearheaded by Tomlinson.

He led the league in rushing with 1,815 yards. He scored 31 touchdowns, his 28 rushing ones still an NFL record. Heck, he even threw two touchdown passes.

But as much as Chargers boosters remember the season, they curse it.

The streaking Chargers had earned the AFC's top seed. Talk of Schottenheimer's heartbreaking playoff luck finally changing was constant. Ditto the Chargers making their second Super Bowl ever.

It looked like both goals were taking a first step when the Chargers led the Patriots late in an AFC Divisional playoff game.

Tomlinson had rushed for two touchdowns and 123 yards and caught two passes for 64 yards and it appeared the Chargers would stay undefeated at home.

When Marlon McCree intercepted a late Tom Brady pass, the Chargers were heading to the AFC Championship Game.

Or so they thought before Brady led the Patriots to 11 points in four minutes to steal the win. It ran Schottenheimer's playoff record to 5–13 and the loss cost him his job.

The organizational shakeup came because McCree didn't fall on the ball after the interception, which would have let the Chargers, with Tomlinson, ice the game by draining the clock.

Instead McCree headed upfield and was stripped of the ball by Troy Brown. The Patriots recovered and rallied for a 24–21 victory.

The Chargers reached the AFC Championship Game the following season, but fell again to the Patriots, with a knee injury forcing Tomlinson to the sidelines after two carries.

Tomlinson played two more seasons with the Chargers before ending his career with another two seasons with the Jets.

It's clear, though, where Tomlinson's allegiance lies.

"I will always be a San Diego Charger," he stressed. "I'll bleed blue and gold for the rest of my life."

When leaving the Chargers after the 2009 season, Tomlinson's parting was sour after attempts at negotiations with general manager A. J. Smith.

But Chargers owner Dean Spanos promised Tomlinson he would return in good graces. Tomlinson did when he signed a one-day Chargers contract before making his retirement official in 2012.

Tomlinson's No. 21 was immortalized in 2015, hung in the Qualcomm Stadium rafters. It reminded Tomlinson's teammates of them lifting him after he set the touchdown record.

"The plan was always for me to come back and retire as a San Diego Charger," Tomlinson said. "But you don't think about having your number retired, especially with the greats of Dan Fouts, Lance Alworth, and Junior Seau. For me, it is amazing."

For years, that's just how people explained Tomlinson's running.

While his pace slowed, he's quick to dust off his Chargers recollections when seeing familiar faces as an NFL Network analyst.

"We always talk about the memories that we all shared once, especially now that we are getting old and we are starting to get gray hair," he said. "So it is fun to be around your teammates and reminisce. We have old stories we talk about.

"When I see Philip [Rivers] and [Antonio] Gates, and it just takes me back. Even the bus rides home from games. Those are the things that you cherish and you miss."

Chapter 20

DONNIE EDWARDS

Patriots at Chargers—January 14, 2007

BIRTH DATE:	April 6, 1973
HOMETOWN:	San Diego, California
RESIDENCE:	Rancho Santa Fe, California
JERSEY NO.:	59
POSITION:	Linebacker
HEIGHT:	6-foot-3
WEIGHT:	225 pounds

The Run-up

The phone in the Edwards's San Diego home rang and a skinny linebacker named "Donnie" reached for it.

"We're coming to San Diego right now," UCLA coach Terry Donahue said, with an unmistakable urgency in his tone.

Maybe he was tempted, but Donnie Edwards didn't reply with a "What took you so long?"

Edwards was a star at Chula Vista High School, but he was far from the big man on campus. To be blunt, Edwards stood tall on the field but was light in the pockets.

He checked in right around 170 pounds and on his 6-foot-3 frame, he looked more like an exclamation point than someone to get excited about.

Despite his stellar play, his name didn't get called often by the top-notch college programs.

"I was pretty small," Edwards said. "There weren't a lot of Division I schools that were interested."

Edwards checked most of the school's boxes on what they were seeking—production, athleticism, determination, leadership. But when Edwards hit the scale, it didn't tip in his favor.

"That is exactly where my drive came from, all the negative things that I heard," Edwards said. "I wasn't strong enough. I was too skinny. I wasn't big enough. All those things pushed me."

So he kept getting nudged off the recruiters' list.

He visited UCLA, and considering Donahue himself was an undersized defensive tackle on the Bruins team that upset Michigan State in the 1966 Rose Bowl, the UCLA coach was intrigued by the agile Edwards.

Trouble was, there weren't any scholarships available.

Edwards took a trip to Nebraska, but while there was plenty of corn there, wasn't much coin. Coach Tom Osborne offered to pay for his books and that was it.

"I wanted to show them that I can play," Edwards said. "I knew I was always a good player and that I would hold up."

The only reason Edwards landed on the Bruins' radar was because of Rick Neuheisel. He came to San Diego to scout other players, but he couldn't keep his eyes off the scrawny but scrappy Edwards. But it was so late in the recruiting process that there were no scholarship goodies on the table left for Edwards.

So while his heart was set on going to Westwood, Edwards started considering San Diego State.

"Al Luginbill, the coach there, he really liked me a lot and believed in me," Edwards said. "UCLA was talking to me, but it couldn't offer me a scholarship."

Edwards figured his blue-and-gold ship had set sail when the phone rang at the Edwards's residence.

"A day before the signing date, while I was all gung-ho to go to San Diego State, I got a phone call from UCLA," Edwards said. "Terry and Rick said they were coming to San Diego right now. I said, 'Oh, what do you want?'"

It was a question Edwards asked while praying for the right reply.

"We need to know, right now, if you will come to UCLA," Donahue said.

Edwards grinned when he was told another recruit had reneged on the Bruins. So with an unexpected scholarship, the last scholarship, Donahue offered it to that undersized linebacker reminding him of well, himself.

Edwards, of course, said "Yes" nearly before Donahue could finish with the question.

"Two and a half hours later they were in my living room," Edwards said. "And we are signing the papers."

But Edwards's signature didn't come with a guarantee. At 6-foot-2, 175 pounds he would have to go about proving the doubters wrong.

Edwards had to compensate with his brain and energy for what he lacked in brawn.

"That's how I made a lot of plays." he said. "I would anticipate something, I was ready for it. When I would see the flick of a guard going one way, I would be on it. I wouldn't hesitate and be stepping in the bucket and backing up.

"Instead I wanted to make every tackle. On my side, on someone else's side. I would just go make the tackle and I did that by running and hustling my butt off to try and make every tackle.

"But playing smart is what I absolutely prided myself on and I'm proud to be a UCLA graduate and to get my master's in education there, too. A lot of UCLA Bruins no matter what team they played on when I got to the pros, we felt like we were the smartest players on the field.

"Playing that way allowed me to understand and to anticipate plays, schemes, and the whole concept of what the game was about. I would be looking at formations and be able to anticipate where the plays were going."

Edwards sprinted to a lofty status at UCLA, when he tied a school record with 4.5 sacks against Southern Methodist University. But he couldn't outrun the thought of many who still pegged him as too small.

Not until the Kansas City Chiefs burned a fourth-round draft pick on Edwards in 1996 was his name called for the NFL.

"A 225-pound linebacker, really?" Edwards said of what he heard.

It was a familiar refrain for Edwards.

"They said I was not going to hold up and I defied all the naysayers," he said. "I made it a point to take care of my body and to work harder than everyone else.

"I was only 225 pounds, but I was one of the stronger guys because I lived in the weight room. I knew what I lacked in sheer size I had to compensate for with strength.

"I can't control being 225 pounds; my body frame was not going to hold much more than that. But I lifted a lot of weights and I was strong."

Which made that argument of him being undersized pretty weak.

The Game

By Donnie Edwards

It has to be the 2006 divisional playoff game against the New England Patriots. That's really the game for me, honestly.

I thought this was going to be the year for us, for [coach] Marty [Schottenheimer], for everyone.

Everything was clicking on all cylinders on offense and the defense was playing lights out. Kassim Osgood was crushing it on kickoffs and punts. Just everyone was clicking going into that game.

We had a bye, we were playing at home and we were confident we could beat them.

But at the same time we knew the Patriots were a very experienced team in the postseason. We would definitely have to play our game and not make mistakes, not turn the ball over . . . that kind of stuff.

But unfortunately with the turnover and everything else, and them having Tom Brady, that was too much.

We wanted to put pressure on Brady. [Defensive coordinator] Wade Phillips wanted to go after him. And it may come from this side or that side, but we were going to come after Brady from every direction to make him antsy in the pocket.

I know they were worried about that. I think we were leading the league in sacks that year; Shawne Merriman had 17.

So that was the game plan going in. And the defense was playing well all year, so it didn't really matter who we were going to face.

We could get pressure with just our base defense—three, four defenders was enough pressure by itself. And the way Wade's defenses are there is always pressure; because even in the 3–4 you would have a fourth or fifth guy coming from the right, or the left or right up the middle. Or he would drop the two outside backers and send the two guys up the middle. You just never knew where the rush was coming from.

But I remember in the third quarter we had stopped them on third-and-13. We are heading off the field and this was a big one: Drayton Florence head-butted tight end Daniel Graham and got an unsportsmanlike conduct penalty and they got a whole new series of fresh downs.

I'm thinking, *No, no, no. I had definitely been here before and this was not good.*

I went to Drayton and said, "Are you freaking kidding me?" We were getting ready to give our offense the ball and he head-butted Graham. We got into a tussle on the sidelines. He tried to fight me back and Jamal Williams had to come over and push him off the field, I remember that.

But that is what happens to a guy when he loses his composure and discipline. That was a major setback for us defensively.

Of course they now go down the field and Brady picks us apart and they score again. Now we are leading 14–13 after [Stephen] Gostkowski's field goal.

But we go ahead 21–13 when L. T. [LaDainian Tomlinson] scored a touchdown with eight minutes to play and then we kicked it off to Reche Caldwell. I remember Reche, who had been released by us, had the game of his life.

He was an amazing athlete and when it's playoff time and it's either win or lose and the loser goes home, well he really stepped up. I know he wanted to have a good game against us. No matter what player, after he leaves a team, he wants to have a good game against his former team. And he was revved up and ready to play. He was just so wide open on some big plays.

We intercepted Brady three times, I had one, and the last one was the big one late in the fourth quarter on fourth down.

Marlon McCree got it and all he had to do was fall on the ball, or take a knee and we would run out the clock; we had an eight-point lead. We had L. T., who was the MVP that year, and instead we gave it right back to them.

When McCree caught the ball I was yelling, "Down, down down." I was thinking, *Don't try to run it back.* But it was too late; they were already covering up the ball. Troy Brown had stripped it from McCree and guess who recovered it? Yep, Reche Caldwell.

I was so out of it at that point. I was thinking, *Oh my gosh. I can't believe it. I can't believe it. I can't believe it.*

I don't know what it was about my career, but I never won a playoff game. Never, never, never in fourteen years.

All he had to do was to fall down or even one of our guys could hit him. But he tried to take it back.

You can't do that against guys who know how to win games.

So Caldwell scores on a pass from Brady and they go for two points with four minutes or so to go. It was a shotgun play and Kevin [Faulk] was offset a bit in the backfield. Knowing Brady, what we were thinking and anticipating was a quick pass. Maybe a little throw on a stick route to the tight end or something quick out in the flat to Faulk and he outruns the outside linebacker to the end zone.

All we had to do was stop them on either of those plays and we win the game.

Instead they shoot a direct snap to Faulk and he runs up the middle for two points and the game is tied, 21–21.

When I think about it I remember telling the guys on the sidelines that we know how to win, we had been winning all year. All those games that we played we always found a way to win. That is what good teams do so often is that they find a way to win. Someone will make a play, someone has to make a stop. That is what we had done all year and we were confident.

We were 14–2 and the confidence was there. It didn't matter if we were at home or away, regular season or preseason. We expected to win, so let's go make a play on the last drive.

But you never can bet against Brady.

Caldwell got so wide open for 49 yards and Gostkowski kicked another field goal. They take a 24–21 lead with a minute left.

We try a field goal from 54 yards and Nate Kaeding missed. I just thought, *Oh my gosh!*

I remember Eric Parker had one of the worst days of his career when he muffed a couple of punts.

I remember Drayton Florence and his head-butt.

I remember Shaun Phillips almost recovered a fumble.

And then Marlon's play.

But it wasn't Marlon's fault that we lost the game. There was a whole bunch of errors. We had four turnovers and it seemed every time we made a mistake they would make us pay for it and that was what happened.

It was so unfortunate.

As a team, we had so many missed opportunities. If we just recover one of those fumbles, if Parker doesn't muff those punts, if Kaeding didn't miss a field goal, if Marlon just falls down. Or if we stop them on the two-point conversion.

There were just so many opportunities and all we had to do was just be successful on one of them and we would have won that game.

We absolutely thought we were going to the Super Bowl that year. L. T. was incredible that year. The offense was so good they would go down and score so fast we would think, *Would you not score so damn fast so we could catch our breath*. But really that was just a great team.

It was so fun competing and there was a great camaraderie. We were really close and had a lot of fun together. We were winning and everybody was on board. When you are winning it's a lot easier for it to be that way; what good memories.

It was a special time and a special team and that was the year where it could have been. There was no way we weren't going to the Super Bowl—we thought that 100 percent. And I think everybody else thought that as well.

But that was the last game I ever suited up as a Charger. I didn't get an opportunity to stay a Charger. Marty got fired. After that game, just too many egos got in the way.

The Aftermath

Donnie Edwards played on one of the most dynamic teams in Chargers history. That 2006 squad that fell to the New England Patriots in the playoffs was stacked.

In fact, years later then-New York Jets coach Rex Ryan confirmed it. Ryan was on a conference call with the media covering the Chargers and was asked what would have happened if he would had been hired as head coach in 2007, instead of Norv Turner. Ryan was a finalist for the position after Marty Schottenheimer was fired despite going 14–2 in 2006.

"Oh we would have won a couple of Super Bowls," Ryan said. "Those teams were loaded."

But Edwards, who came to the Chargers as a free agent, was unloaded after the 2006 season, a season in which the Chargers not only won 14 of 16 games but finished the year with a 10-game winning streak. That Chargers bunch not only had the NFL MVP in LaDainian Tomlinson, but boasted of possessing five All-Pro and nine Pro-Bowl players.

But, like so often in the NFL, players and coaches went in different directions after the shocking meltdown against the Patriots.

Some went home for good.

Edwards left his native city to a place he considered his old stomping grounds.

"I was kind of like Dorothy in the *Wizard of Oz*," Edwards said. "You know, there's no place like home."

Edwards, born in San Diego, was raised professionally in Kansas City. So following the heartbreak of not being invited back by the Chargers, he was welcomed again in the heartland.

"It was cool," Edwards said. "Kansas City was the team and the city that adopted me back when I was twenty-two years old and a fourth-round pick out of UCLA. I spent six years there before I had the opportunity to go to San Diego.

"When I didn't get a contract offer from the Chargers, I still wanted to play. The Chiefs were the team that was really lobbying to get me there."

It wasn't too tough of a sell. Edwards knew of that special connection between the Chiefs and their fans.

"Playing in Kansas City is great, different from a lot of other pro teams," he said. "It's almost like a college atmosphere where everyone in the whole entire city is all about the team. The team and the community are synonymous with each other. We know them, they know us. They support you, through thick and thin. The kind of fans that are really true hard-core dedicated fans. They know their football 100 percent."

That point couldn't be underestimated. Same went with playing in Arrowhead Stadium.

"It is pretty special," he said. "The fans are right there behind the bench, I mean right there. At Qualcomm Stadium, the closest ones are 50, 60 yards away. At Arrowhead it is this close, intimate feeling."

Edwards was also still seeking his first postseason victory. He evaluated the Chiefs' roster and recent history and decided his chances were good for a playoff run.

"They had hired Herm Edwards and they had a pretty good team," he said. "They went to the playoffs the year before and I thought it was a great opportunity."

When 2007 rolled around, Edwards and his new teammates were ready to rock.

"We had really high hopes to have a great team," he said. "I thought this was going to be a great way to finish out my career. I was hoping for this great ending and it didn't go as planned."

Edwards was brought in, but the team gutted its roster of most of its veteran players. Youth was being served in a big portion and all it provided was a season-long dose of indigestion.

A year removed from being atop the AFC heap with the 14–2 Chargers, Edwards endured the agony of a 4–12 season.

"The next year was about the same, 2–14, and it was time for a coaching change," Edwards said.

The durable Edwards—he once started 150 consecutive games—was battling injuries his final year. But his torn quad muscle had healed and he wanted to return to the Chiefs. New coach Todd Haley was looking to get even younger, though, and Edwards was the odd man out.

"They told me they were going to rebuild and I had been hurt," Edwards said. "I wanted to keep playing because all I knew was playing football."

He considered an offer by the Oakland Raiders but decided against it. The time had come to bow out, and Edwards exited on his own terms.

"The body was in pretty good shape," he said. "But things change when you get older in how teams look at you."

Edwards, again, really did go home. He pointed his compass to San Diego and away from the NFL.

Before leaving he not only notched 1,000 tackles but joined an exclusive 20/20 club: Edwards finished with 23.5 sacks and 28 interceptions.

"I figured I had a great career and came out of it relatively healthy," he said. "Obviously I would have loved to win a championship and I came close to sniffing it a few times. That is what every kid, that is what all of us play for."

Chapter 21

NICK HARDWICK

Colts at Chargers—January 3, 2009

BIRTH DATE:	September 2, 1981
HOMETOWN:	Indianapolis, Indiana
RESIDENCE:	Point Loma, California
JERSEY NO.:	61
POSITION:	Center
HEIGHT:	6-foot-4
WEIGHT:	295 pounds

The Run-up

As an undersized teenager, Nick Hardwick sized up prep football and came to this conclusion: no thanks.

"I was under 5-foot-4, 125 pounds and I didn't think football was going to be in the cards for me," he said. "I loved the sport and won the trophy in the eighth grade for the hardest hit, but I was this little, tiny guy. I hadn't even hit puberty yet, didn't even have hair under my armpits.

"I didn't play hardly at all. I sat on the bench and watched the guys and thought, *This is not very fun.*"

So Hardwick went from gathering splinters to pinning guys on the mat. Hardwick turned to wrestling, and on flipped a switch as he upended one rival after another.

"I fell in love with it," he said. "And the wrestling coaches were mentors and leaders for me. They were tough, they were serious, and I needed that at that point in my life. It was a perfect fit. We worked hard and everything else fell away from me. I only had room in my head for wrestling."

Hardwick became a state champion before matriculating at the state's biggest university. He entered Purdue, putting sports behind him as he embraced the college lifestyle.

But Hardwick became a Boilermaker just as Purdue's football team became red hot.

"I had never been part of big-time football or went to big-time games," said Hardwick, an Indianapolis native. "The Colts were not very good and I wasn't into them and they were not that important.

"I get to Purdue and there is a madness around the college campus on game days and I had never been a part of that. You go to the games and there are 70,000 people going bananas for this Drew Brees-led team. I'm sitting 50 rows above the field, screaming and yelling and being part of it."

But another part of Hardwick itched to be between the lines.

"I had always been the center of attention, so for me to be cheering for someone else was kind of weird," he said. "The competitive nature in me said I could be playing. If nothing else, I would have a better seat being down on the field. But I knew I could do something to help the football team."

Hardwick later spotted an announcement in the student paper for walk-on tryouts. Hardwick and two of his Marine Corps ROTC colleagues decided to give football a go with the rest of the has-beens and wanna-bes.

"Five of us made the football team and I was the only one to stick past a year; the other ones fell out," Hardwick said. "Man, those 6:00 a.m. workouts were brutal."

Then-coach Joe Tiller had lost Brees and other stars to graduation. Tiller figured to compensate, he had to have the most well-conditioned team this side of the US Army.

"Those 6:00 a.m. workouts were the hardest thing I ever did," said Hardwick, and yes, that includes the NFL. "It was unbelievable and I didn't think I was going to make it through spring. At one point I was running and was hyperventilating and I looked at a coach and said, 'I can't breathe.' The coach looked at me and said, 'That is too bad and the door is over there. Or you can just get on the line and run again.' I got on the line, but I think I got an ulcer doing those workouts. I know my grade-point average dropped three points in the matter of six weeks during my last year. But I stuck it out."

The next year, someone was sticking his hand out at Chargers Park.

"I ended up being drafted by San Diego and the first day, I'm sitting in that makeshift cafeteria eating lunch before practice," Hardwick said. "Someone taps me on the shoulder and says, 'Hey Boilermaker.' I look up and holy [crap] it's Drew Brees!

"I thought, *this is unbelievable*, because he was really the inspiration for why I wanted to play in the first place. If he is not at Purdue and hadn't created the frenzy in West Lafayette and made it so maddening around campus, I wouldn't have played.

"And for him to sit down and have lunch with me, I thought my life was complete. I was living a dream."

The Game

By Nick Hardwick

The one that really stands out to me is the playoff game at home against Indianapolis at the end of the 2008 season.

Because that whole deal before it was trying to finish the season 8–8 and make the playoffs. It was unbelievable, the highs and lows of that season. It was nothing like I had every played in before or since. It was ridiculous.

You have to remember what it was like just getting to that game.

We were 3–3, went to Buffalo and lost in Buffalo, and that took us to 3–4. We all expected to win there and it didn't happen for whatever reason.

After the Buffalo game we were going to London to play the Saints. We go straight to the airport and we were delayed for two hours.

So we were crammed in this little airport bar, almost every player on the team, and drank all the beer and ate all the food they had. It was packed. It turned into quite a party. We knew we were 3–4, but we knew we had a decent team but we just couldn't put it together.

So we're in the bar toasting to nine straight wins—that was what we were going to do. Of course we go to London and lose to the Saints.

So we changed the toast on the way home to winning eight games. Of course we come home to a bye, then lose the next four games.

We ended up needing four straight wins to end the season to give ourselves a chance to go 8–8 and make the playoffs.

In Week 16 after our 15th game, we beat Tampa Bay and are coming back home on the plane. Denver is playing the Bills in Denver and Buffalo beats them and that surprised the crap out of everybody. When they announced the score on the plane, it just erupts. People were taking their shirts off, running up and down the aisle. It was crazy.

We are playing Denver next week at home and we know, undoubtedly, we are going to beat them. And we beat the tar out of them (52–21) and think, *Oh my gosh, this is a season of destiny. It is working out like it is supposed to for us.*

So Indy comes in for the playoff game at 11–5 and we knew that we had its number. And it was a battle, a heck of a playoff game. We won 23–17.

It was just a matchup that was favorable for us because of our size and speed.

They were a smaller football team and a lot of the times playing teams with big guys they were really elusive. But we were kind of middle of the road in size, but at the same time we were really strong and really fast. That matchup worked really well for us because we had the speed to combat them and we had really good, athletic players.

I just remember the game was close, it was back and forth, and then all of a sudden we're in overtime and we got the ball and it didn't take long. Darren Sproles caught the edge of the defense and I knew it was over.

Guys were celebrating, running up and down the field. I wanted to take my pads off. I wanted to get naked. Because I just had too much energy inside my body.

It was an isolation running play and Darren ended up bouncing it outside. Jacob Hester was the lead blocker and we were just working the oldest play possible—running the isolation play at the middle linebacker—and Sproles took it in from there from 22 yards.

And for him to make it happen, it was unbelievable because it wrapped up that whole season. It was the highest of highs and the lowest of lows, but we only got to that high because we had been so down that year.

We were 4–8 at one point and it looked like it wasn't ever going to happen. And we turned that around. We had a little luck and we capitalized on that. That was the most fun I ever had. I had never felt that good in my life. It was the most euphoric feeling I had ever had.

The Aftermath

It was summertime and the weather was right. Nick Hardwick was right where he wanted to be: Plopping on the pads at the Chargers' 2014 training camp.

"Being in the locker room with a bunch of guys and getting ready for practice," he said. "And just knowing you would get to fight on a daily basis. It was like fighting my brothers and trying to be a tough kid and growing up into being a tough man. Man, I was living the dream."

There's that description of what playing in the NFL meant to Hardwick. The other one is a tad coarse.

"Wake up, [pass gas], and fight," he said. "It doesn't get any better than that; it was unbelievable."

But reality has its ugly way of breaking up bodies and demolishing dreams.

"My body was starting to break down, my neck in particular," said Hardwick, a member of the Chargers' 50th anniversary team "It was just an accumulation of being beat down, nonstop. I had so many stingers over the course of my career that I could never get comfortable."

Hardwick got through camp but the sensation of bee stings in his triceps rode along, too. The feeling in his hands was inconsistent, which meant some days he couldn't open a post-practice bottle of water.

That wasn't the only clue, as Hardwick suddenly preferred shirts he could just slip over his neck.

"I had trouble buttoning my shirts," he said. "Everyday functions became harder and harder."

But there was Hardwick, trotting out with the first unit for the 2014 season opener. Nothing shocking about that: during the previous four seasons, Hardwick never missed a start and seldom skipped a snap.

That first game, though, came with an injury. Hardwick's ankle had buckled but no one gave it much of a thought. In 2009, he was out 13 games with a severe ankle injury, before coming back probably too early for the team's playoff push.

But this was more than an ankle injury. Hardwick couldn't shake the stingers or the sensation that his body was revolting from this most violent of a game.

"I gave it that one last go, had a good camp, and got my body in shape, but the stingers were just out of control," he said. "It was time to knock it off."

He would play in the opener on September 8 but didn't make it to halftime. When he left the field that Monday night at University of Phoenix Stadium he would never rise again as a football player.

Two days later he was placed on injured reserved. Fast-forward months later and he confirmed what everyone speculated after he shed numerous pounds while shedding a few tears. Hardwick announced his retirement on February 2, 2015.

"My neck was the final straw that broke the camel's back," he said. "You learn from the guys that had to step away before you and take all the information in. You just try to do what is the best for you and right for you."

To his left on those great Chargers lines was Kris Dielman. Like Hardwick, he was chased from the game prematurely, both because of injuries above their shoulders.

"It was time to step aside and make a very tough, but mature decision," Hardwick said.

That step kept him on the sidelines, now as a Chargers radio reporter. Although some former rivals would have trouble recognizing Hardwick after he shed 70 pounds, the one-time undersized center at 295 pounds looked just right at 225.

"I was never a big man and it was a real struggle even for me to get to 290 and maintain it through the season," Hardwick said. "I remember at the end of my second year I was at 268. You don't find a lot of guys playing center in the NFL under 270 pounds."

By going smaller, Hardwick also crossed the mental bridge that he would no longer stand tall among the massive bodies.

"I wanted to take off that suit of armor that I had on, so mentally I couldn't think that I could still get out there," he said. "Being at 225 pounds, it was clear I can't do that anymore. It's just not possible."

He did the impossible, in many people's eyes, by lasting 11 seasons.

"My God was it a blast, everything about it," he said. "It was terrifying, scary, mundane, and it was just the time of my life. I can say right now that I would not have taken any of it back. It was too good of a time."